Theodor W. Adorno

an introduction

Post-Contemporary Interventions

Contents

Preface to the English Edition vii

Translator's Preface xi

1   The Project of Renewing Childhood by Transforming One's Life 1

2   Critical Theory 11

3   Reason's Self-Criticism 18
    Defined Negation 20
    The Two Faces of Enlightenment 26

4   Rescuing What is Beyond Hope 34
    Philosophy from the Perspective of Redemption 34
    Primacy of the Object 38

5   The Totally Socialized Society 51
    The Concept of Society 52
    Liquidation of the Individual 58
    Critical Theory on Morality 68

6   The Goal of the Emancipated Society   77

7   The Powerless Utopia of Beauty   91
The Destruction and Salvation of Art   93
The Silence of Music   102
The Transition from Art to Knowledge   109
Theorizing Art and Culture in the Institute for Social Research   112
Benjamin and Kracauer: Theorizing Mass Art   120
Anarchistic and Bourgeois Romanticism: Adorno's Critique of Benjamin   125
The Work of Art and the Concept of Truth   128

8   The Failure of Culture   136
The Radically Pathetic and Guilty Culture   137
Enlightenment as Mass Deception   144

Biographical Timeline   159

Notes   163

Bibliography   171

Index   179

Preface to
the English Edition

THIS BOOK AIMS TO PRESENT some of the main motifs of Adorno's critical theory in a concise and clear manner. The presentation starts from the core concepts of his philosophy and shows how they are developed in the framework of sociology as well as that of aesthetic and cultural theory. I refer constantly to Adorno's *Minima Moralia* and his *Negative Dialectics*: together with his contribution to *Dialectic of Enlightenment*, these constitute, when we think of his work systemically, his most important achievements. From this perspective I have outlined the thought patterns I see as essential, as sustaining and shaping the complex and highly differentiated structure of Adorno's philosophy. Inevitably I have neglected elements which would surely be essential to a comprehensive portrayal of Adorno's multilayered thinking. And I have not been able to do full justice to the multifaceted dimensions of the history of thought, in which Adorno's intellectual odyssey is embedded.

This odyssey begins with neo-Kantian positions, moving through a preoccupation with Husserl's phenomenology—decisively influenced by the philosophical avant-garde of Lukács, Bloch, and Benjamin—to an engagement with Freud and Kierkegaard. Adorno's intellectual journey leads him to Hegel, Marx, and Nietzsche, and later culminates in his critique of Heidegger, but always ultimately permits him to return to Kant. Not all of this is reconstructed here; where necessary, it can be read back into the intellectual outcomes. Moreover, experts in music theory will hardly be satisfied with the brevity with which I have discussed Adorno's philosophy of music, while for lay people too many questions in this field will remain open.

My decision to weight matters in this way reflects the fact that this book is intended as a philosophical introduction to Adorno's thought, not as a comprehensive portrayal of the theoretical cosmos of a thinker who today is often called the last universal genius. Recent monographs in German are available that portray him in his entirety; particularly noteworthy is Detlev Claussen's study, published in 2003, the year of Adorno's centenary. I hope that my more selective portrayal will help render accessible Adorno's thinking, which is consistently critical of systems but in no way unsystematic. My study concentrates on a series of core philosophical concepts, using these as a base from which to trace Adorno's perspective when he deploys these concepts in fields such as the aesthetics of music and literature. The web of philosophical history into which Adorno's thinking opens—he gave life and power to the history of ideas in a way matched by few twentieth-century thinkers—is here brought to life only indirectly. But it is present as a subtext. This allusive method has found resonance among German-speaking readers, thereby seeming to justify my methodological decision.

For the present English-language edition I have expanded the text in several places. I have incorporated thinking from three essays that I first published in 2003 and 2005, in the *Zeitschrift für kritische Theorie* and in the collection *Modelle kritischer Gesellschaftstheorie*.

At this point I would like to thank my father, Hermann Schweppenhäuser, for his multifaceted introduction, over many years, to critical theory. I wish to acknowledge with gratitude how important reading *Negative Dialectics* with Sven Kramer in the late 1980s has been for my interpretation of Adorno. And I thank Herbert Schnädelbach, with whom I studied philosophy in Hamburg in the 1980s, for inviting me in 1995 to write this book for the series of "introductory" volumes he directed at Hamburg's Junius-Verlag. Another contributor to this constellation was the philosopher Detlef Horster from Hanover, also a member of the advisory board for the Hamburg series, who has been my friend since my participation in the philosophy seminar at the University of Hanover. To Fredric Jameson, with whom I have had many conversations during and since my time as visiting professor in Duke University's literature program, I owe insights into new ways of reading and contextualizing Adorno's aesthetics and cultural theory. And I am especially glad that James Rolleston has taken on the task of translating the book; with him I know my text is in good hands.

GERHARD SCHWEPPENHÄUSER
Weimar, July 2006

Translator's Preface

DOES THEODOR ADORNO STILL NEED to be introduced? Arguably, he always will, not because he is an obscure figure, but for almost the opposite reason: he may be the last great intellectual whose aim was to synthesize the essential insights of Western philosophy in the interest of a critical social and political perspective. His predecessors in this modern German tradition—Kant, Hegel, Marx, Nietzsche, Walter Benjamin—give an idea of what to expect in Adorno's work. His goal was to revisit their ethical and sociological arguments in light of two enormous twentieth-century experiences: the rise of fascism, culminating in the Holocaust, and the standardizing of "popular" culture as a commodity indispensable to contemporary capitalism. Adorno's early training in musicology gave him unique, often controversial insights into the latter phenomenon.

So wide-ranging were the critical tasks he set himself that Adorno's prose could become necessarily complex. Gerhard Schweppenhäuser has done a magisterial job of elucidating the core elements of

Adorno's thinking. My decision as translator has been to provide my own versions of the direct citations from Adorno. I sought thereby to generate a linguistic continuum that does justice to both Schweppenhäuser and Adorno himself. With the help of my multitalented assistant, Dell Williams, I have provided, at the end, a list of the works cited, as well as an updated list of scholarly books on Adorno in English.

JAMES ROLLESTON
Durham, July 2008

Theodor W. Adorno

an introduction

1

The Project of Renewing Childhood by Transforming One's Life

IN 1943, WHILE EXILED IN CALIFORNIA, Adorno became personally acquainted with the German author Thomas Mann, whom he greatly admired. As neighbors in Hollywood they became close both socially and professionally. The world-famous, Nobel Prize–winning novelist, who was nearing seventy, initiated the unknown music theorist, who had just turned forty, into his project of writing *the* novel about the dialectic of German culture. In Mann's *Doktor Faustus* the debate focuses on a culture that metamorphoses into an archaic brutality implemented with the most modern technology and methods of violence; this happens not by chance, but on the basis of the structural ambivalence inherent in that culture. In Hollywood, Adorno, through his understanding of music theory, became "coauthor" of Thomas Mann's novel.[1]

In his account of the creation of *Doktor Faustus*, Thomas Mann writes the following about Theodor Ludwig Wiesengrund-Adorno, born in Frankfurt on September 11, 1903:

"His father was a German Jew," namely, Oskar Wiesengrund, a Frankfurt wine wholesaler who had converted to Protestantism; "his mother, herself a singer, is the daughter of a French officer of Corsican —originally Genoan—descent, who married a German singer": Maria, born Maria Cavelli-Adorno della Piana. "Adorno, as he calls himself, using his mother's maiden name, is a person of the same kind of aloof, tragically astute, and exclusive intellectual temperament [as] Walter Benjamin, who, hounded to death by the Nazis, left as a legacy the book on 'German tragic drama'—in reality a philosophy and history of allegory."

Mann continues: "Growing up in an atmosphere totally dominated by theoretical (including political) and aesthetic, above all musical, interests," Adorno achieved, even as a young man, an impressive intellectual impact in liberal Frankfurt. His happy childhood and youth were clouded, if at all, only by the antipathy that narrow-minded fellow students may have shown toward him, a privileged and highly gifted boy. Later, in *Minima Moralia*, he described these "malicious schoolmates" as "messengers" of fascism. Such experiences became the basis of his aversion to "conformist identity," which he had been investigating since the 1940s using innovative methods in the social sciences.

Adorno was trained in philosophy by his older friend Siegfried Kracauer, an important literary journalist at the *Frankfurter Zeitung*: "For several years, every Saturday afternoon, he would read with me the *Critique of Pure Reason*. I don't exaggerate in the slightest when I say that I owe more to these study sessions than I do to my academic instructors."

As a student, Adorno was already an influential music critic in the spirit of radical modernism. He stood up for Schoenberg early on. Some of his own compositions were performed in Frankfurt. At twenty-one he concluded his study of philosophy, musicology, psychology, and sociology by gaining a doctorate in philosophy with Hans Cornelius. Cornelius was also the teacher and patron of Max Horkheimer, later the director of the Frankfurt Institute for Social

Research and founder of critical theory as a standpoint for social analysis. In 1925 Adorno went to Vienna for a year. We read in Mann's account:

> This strange intellect persisted in a lifelong refusal to choose professionally between philosophy and music. It was all too clear to him that he was really pursuing the same goals in the two divergent fields. His dialectical way of thinking and his immersion in the philosophy of society and history—these traits are inseparable from his musical passion. Adorno pursued this passion in his studies of piano and composition with Alban Berg and Eduard Steuermann in Vienna. From 1928 to 1931, as editor of the Viennese journal *Anbruch* [Dawn], he worked on behalf of radical modernist music.

Back in Frankfurt, Adorno intensified his contact with the Institute for Social Research, linked as he was to Max Horkheimer, its director, by theoretical interests they had shared since their time at university. Adorno described their first meeting later in an "Open letter to Max Horkheimer" on the latter's seventieth birthday:

> When I first saw you, in Adhemar Gelb's psychology seminar, since you are eight years older you hardly looked like a student to me; rather, I saw you as a young gentleman from a prosperous family, evincing a certain distanced interest in science. You were untouched by the academic's vocational deformation that leads him all too easily to confuse an involvement in learned matters with reality itself. Yet what you said was so clever, so astute, and above all so independent-minded, that I quickly began seeing you as superior to that sphere from which you held yourself imperceptibly aloof.

A main theme of the institute's work was research into the causes of the unfolding self-dissolution of bourgeois society that was to lead, in Germany, to the authoritarian state. In order to comprehend why human subjects submitted to domination against their own interests, and indeed identified with their rulers, Horkheimer's critical theory linked insights from Marx to a form of psychoanalysis progressively developed into a social psychology, and began to integrate into its investigations the methodology of empirical social research, barely known in Germany at that point. In Horkheimer's institute, philosophy had the task of systematically fusing the interdisciplinary, largely empirical studies focused on this core theme into a materialist theory of the social revolution that had not occurred; the goal was to be able to contribute to such a revolution, to the extent it remained feasible.

Together with Herbert Marcuse, Leo Löwenthal, Erich Fromm, and others, Adorno as a music theorist worked in this context on an interdisciplinary theory of the overall social process, grounded in a critique of ideology. He investigated the social content of music in order to gain information about the dual character of artworks, understood by him as both autonomous constructs and socially determined products. He revealed the social content of music not from the outside, as something sociologically given, but through analysis of the formal aesthetic structuring of the works themselves. Adorno combined musicological analyses with sociological investigations of both the ways society shapes music and the public impacts of its production, reception, and distribution. Thus from his special field, music, he could gain insights into the social totality. At the same time, stimulated by Ernst Bloch and Georg Lukács, and in a productive exchange with his teacher and friend Walter Benjamin, Adorno worked to articulate, in his dissertation on Kierkegaard, the social and potentially critical content of philosophy.

Adorno had met Benjamin in 1923, when Kracauer introduced them. "I saw Benjamin quite frequently, I'd say at least once a week, probably more often, during the whole time he lived in France," Adorno later wrote. "Later I also saw him regularly, not only on his visits here but above all in Berlin. I was very young then and he was eleven years older; I very much felt myself to be the apprentice. I know that I listened to him with total fascination, sometimes then asking him for more details. Very soon he began showing me some of his writings before they were published."

As Thomas Mann continues the story, in 1931 Adorno "qualified as a lecturer at Frankfurt University, where he taught philosophy until expelled by the Nazis." After that he tried first to "survive the winter" in Germany. At the same time, he sought to gain an academic foothold as an instructor in Oxford. Until 1937 Adorno regularly returned from Oxford to Frankfurt for extended visits. After initial misunderstandings and annoyances he was able, in 1938, to gain clear status as collaborator in the Institute for Social Research and to emigrate to the United States with his wife, the newly graduated doctor of chemistry Margarete Karplus. In Thomas Mann's words: "Since 1941 he has been living in Los Angeles almost as a neighbor." It was there that he changed his name to Theodor W. Adorno.

His ongoing work as a member of the institute's inner circle, which began after his emigration, first to New York and then to Los Angeles, defined not only Adorno's professional life but also his specific experiences of American life. While he never could reconcile himself to American culture, he also knew that he was in a sense indebted to it:

> In America I was liberated from a naïve belief in culture as such; I became able to view culture from outside. To clarify: despite all critiques of society and awareness of the primacy of the economic, I had always assumed as obvious the absolute relevance of the spiritual. In America I learned that this obvious relevance was simply not so: there, there is no silent respect for everything spiritual, such as prevails in Central and Western Europe far beyond the so-called educated classes; the absence of this respect provokes the mind to critical self-reflection.

Just as important for Adorno was "the experience of democratic forms as having substance; . . . they are wired into American life, whereas in Germany they were never more than formal rules of the game—and I'm afraid they're still no more than that." He applied this social experience to a concept, rooted in Marx and Engels, that was already central to him before his emigration: genuine humanism.

> Over there I came to recognize a potential for genuine humanness such as can hardly be found in old Europe. The political forms of democracy are just infinitely closer to people. Notwithstanding the much deplored haste, there is in American daily life an element of peace, benevolence, and generosity that is totally remote from the pent-up malice and resentment that erupted in Germany between 1933 and 1945. . . . In German sociological studies one constantly encounters statements by subjects that go: "We're not yet mature

enough for democracy"; such expressions of simultaneous urge to dominate and self-hatred are hard to imagine in the supposedly so much younger world. By that I don't mean to say that America is inoculated against such a collapse into totalitarian power structures.

Adorno sought to demonstrate this danger by using the methods of empirical social research in his studies of the authoritarian personality. "The danger of authoritarianism is inherent in the core tendency of modern society," he wrote. "But the power to resist fascist impulses is probably stronger in America than in any European country, with the possible exception of England." With his critique of the American culture industry, which anticipated the European and subsequently worldwide mechanisms of mass culture, and especially with his pathbreaking *Studies of the Authoritarian Personality*, published in the United States in 1950, Adorno contributed, as an immigrant, to the insights of democratic society into its own ambivalence. According to Adorno, the inner contradiction of culture lies in the way it promises human fullness on the basis of an inhuman, repressive social formation; ultimately culture negates its own promise by surrendering entirely, as culture industry, to the rules of commodity production. And it is no mere accident of biography that his investigation into the authoritarian character took place in the most democratic country. The self-undermining tendency of democratic society became open to empirical social-psychological analysis for the first time through the well-known "F-scale," presented in Adorno's studies into the authoritarian character. This scale measured the character dispositions that make individuals "especially receptive to antidemocratic propaganda."

In the United States, then, Adorno did not only work with Thomas Mann on *Doktor Faustus*, with its inspiration drawn from musical aesthetics. He also wrote the *Essay on Wagner* and *Philosophy of Modern Music*; he produced *Minima Moralia* and *Dialectic of Enlightenment*, the latter written in collaboration with Max Horkheimer. With Horkheimer, Adorno returned to Frankfurt in 1949. The philosophy students there knew little about their new professor, who had just returned from exile. Insiders knew that he had helped Thomas Mann, exiled in California, with the creation of *Dok-

tor Faustus, which had just been published. For many postwar Frankfurt philosophy students, the lectures by Adorno and the other "new" professor, Max Horkheimer (who had also taught in Frankfurt in the 1930s, before the National Socialists drove him and Adorno away), seemed like a revelation. For otherwise, in the philosophy department, philosophy was taught, in the years 1933 to 1945, both in Germany and elsewhere, as if nothing had happened to prevent the subject from being presented, now as before, in the good old academic way.

When Adorno was later asked, at the beginning of the 1960s, why he had returned to Germany, he pointed to the "continuity of his intellectual life" and the dialectical embeddedness of his thinking in the German philosophical tradition. He pointed to "the language which is my own to write in, whereas in the long years as an emigrant I learned to write English, at best, just like everyone else," and to his sense that in Germany he was free from the pressures of the market and of public opinion. He stressed that only a failure to understand the socioeconomic roots of fascism could lead to the view that it was grounded in a supposed German national character; hence the very construction of a "collective guilt" was dubious, belonging to the psychological climate "that produced fascism." He intended to continue his critical theoretical work in the place where his concrete life experience was rooted. He did not want there to be confusion between

> the sense of continuity and fidelity to one's own origins and an obstinacy and arrogance about what one simply is. Fidelity like this means that one would rather try to change something in the place where one's own experience is centered than simply abandon it for a quite different place. I simply wanted to return to the place of my childhood, ultimately on the basis of the feeling that what one achieves in life is nothing other than the attempt to regain one's childhood by transforming it. I did not underestimate the danger and difficulty of my decision, but to this day I have not regretted it.

Beginning in 1949, Adorno held a specially structured professorship in philosophy and the sociology of music at the University of Frankfurt; four years later he became a regular distinguished professor of social philosophy and finally, in 1956, chaired professor of sociology and philosophy. In 1950, together with Horkheimer, he restarted and directed the Institute for Social Research. And there, in the 1950s, critical sociology received its big impetus toward a breakthrough in the Federal Republic.

In the 1960s Adorno became one of the most important critical intellectuals in the young Federal Republic. From 1963 to 1968 he was president of the German sociological society. His essay collections *Prisms*, *Interventions*, and *Catchwords* were influential far beyond the academic sphere. On the radio and in the press he was an active public intellectual who made his points sharply; for example, he strongly advocated the liberalization of laws criminalizing some sexual behaviors.

Adorno waged his primary struggle against forgetting, against a process that, under the name "overcoming the past," was supposed to clear away the final obstacles standing in the way of the restoration and "economic miracle" being produced in the "aligned society." (The concept of the aligned society had been coined by Ludwig Erhard, who in 1963 had succeeded Konrad Adenauer as federal chancellor.) Detlev Claussen writes, "In the last twenty-five years of his life Adorno kept his eyes trained on the afterlife of National Socialism. From the consciousness of the actuality of Auschwitz emerged the consciousness of necessary remembering. Without chasing after actuality, he made it possible for many people to use his intellectual efforts as aids to genuine experience."

His impact was undeniable. In the mid-1960s the Frankfurt School, as it was called by then, attracted attention as a "mentor" of the protest movement. The demonstrations against the Vietnam War, the "operations" of Commune One in Berlin, the killing on June 2, 1967, of the student Benno Ohnesorg, who had been peacefully demonstrating against the state visit of the Shah of Iran, the assassination attempt against Rudi Dutschke in April 1968: all these events affected the political climate of the republic in the following years. It soon became clear that although Adorno and the protest movement generally agreed in their critique of existing society, they differed significantly concerning the means for bringing about change. Adorno expressed public solidarity with the intentions of the student protests, which were directed not only at university reform but also at initiating a public debate over National Socialism. He saw the urgent need for an extraparliamentary opposition, supported the resistance to the emergency laws, and endorsed the student blockade of newspapers published by Axel Springer. But unlike Herbert Marcuse, for example, he rejected all forms of actionism and violence because, in his view, they falsely presented themselves as revolutionary acts. For Adorno, they recalled the antidemocratic potential of some prefascist movements. When, not long before his death, Adorno spoke in a newspaper interview about the possibilities of a radical democratic politics in the Federal Republic, he said, "The decisive point of difference is that, under present-day sociological and technical conditions, transformative praxis is conceivable only as nonviolent and conducted within the framework of the basic law."

In his final years, Adorno's philosophical energy was devoted to the preparation of his last works, *Negative Dialectics* (1966) and *Aesthetic Theory* (unfinished at the time of his death and published posthumously in 1970). Many of his leftist supporters held it against him that he resisted a uniform politics. In this period Adorno was shaken by the disruptions of his teaching carried out by rebellious students; in 1969, alarmed at the prospect of Frankfurt students occupying the Institute for Social Research, he called the police for help. Perhaps the students reminded him of National Socialist shock troops; in any case he was not ready to allow the freely operating institute to be "occupied" again by anyone. In addition, a campaign was instigated against his edition of Walter Benjamin's writings. He was falsely charged with having exploited, during his years of exile, Benjamin's dependence on the institute and with distorting his writings.

In July 1969, his doctoral student Hans-Jürgen Krahl was put on trial in Frankfurt for breach of the peace. Krahl used the occasion to make a malicious attack on Adorno in the courtroom. In one sense, this attack expressed student disappointment that Adorno could see no way of justifying violent individual actions during pseudorevolutionary campaigns. In another sense, the left-wing students' ambivalent attitude toward their professors came into the open: a kind of

Oedipal rebellion was underway. During the student movement very few right-wing professors were attacked and boycotted at German universities; the protesting students preferred to target precisely those academic figures who had taught them to think critically about society.

After Adorno had testified in court, he left Frankfurt for a vacation in Switzerland with his wife. Without taking time to relax and acclimate, he immediately set off on a strenuous hike and suffered a heart attack. In the hospital he seemed not immediately aware of the seriousness of the situation; his wife continued to supply him with reading material, the crime novels that were essential to him. Adorno died on August 6, 1969, in Visp in the canton of Wallis. In the mainstream of Adorno biography, the line is that the revolt of his students against him and his academic friends broke his heart. We now know, from his surviving letters, that the unjust attacks on his editorial methods in the Benjamin edition affected him far more severely. Furthermore, an unhappy love relationship had very recently come to an end, which must have been frustrating for Adorno.

Critical Theory

IN JUNE 1969, ADORNO PUBLISHED an article in the weekly *Die Zeit* in which he reflected on the concept of critical theory and its task both in the public domain and in philosophy. Adorno's strategy in this article is "critical" in a double sense: he engages both the suppression of the critical perspective and its functional deployment, both of which he views as false. He writes, "It seems to me as if the spirit of public critique, since being monopolized by political groups, hence clearly compromised, has suffered severe setbacks; I hope I'm wrong." In this phrasing one senses Adorno's annoyance at how, in discussions of the student revolt, critical theory was constantly reproached for staying out of the political struggle. Adorno sees a variant of the German anticritical tradition at work here, wherein the critic must always display "positive" credentials. As he puts it, apropos of the 1968 demonstrators' cult of action, "The collective pressure for a positive outlook, permitting direct translation into practice, has meanwhile gripped precisely those who see themselves as in acute conflict with society. It is for this reason that their cult of action fits so well into the dominant social trend."

Of course the multiple motivations of the student revolt cannot all be lumped together under the single heading "cult of action." But in this respect Adorno may well have been right. The student movement's cult of action is history; in its place today we see strictly ritualized "actions" that, as components of a "symbolic politics," can be sure of very broad acceptance—from the human chain to the occupation of oil platforms. "Whoever practices critique, without having the power to enforce his opinion, and without installing himself in the public hierarchy, should just shut up": thus does Adorno describe the anti-individualist, power-hungry prejudice that prevails in the political realm today, as it did then. The favorite argument used to silence critics of society is just the same: whoever criticizes must also be able to say how things could be improved. As Adorno notes, Erich Kästner already had to do battle with this argument, in the form of the sanctimonious question about the location of "the positive."

But is that really still the case today? Isn't the standing of critical theory high? Being critical seems to be everyone's goal. "Critical thinking" is an entry requirement for all decent jobs. The "critical consumer" is an elevated concept in the commercial world; a talk-show host who fails to ask critical questions convinces no one (at least in Germany); and "critical capacity" is a civic virtue. But this appearance is deceptive, for criticism that goes to the root of things has a negative image, today just as in the 1970s, when the decree excluding members of extremist organizations from civil-service employment prevailed, providing excuses for barring from public service anyone with politically unpopular opinions. Now as then, the prejudice against criticism that is supposedly merely negative often serves to silence those who draw attention to social evils without simultaneously offering a recipe for change.

But negativity is inherent to critique. Criticizing somebody or something is an act of negation. In that sense, critique indeed has a destructive element. But everyday language contrasts it with "constructive criticism" that is supposed to improve rather than destroy. In German, "constructive" (*konstruktiv*) has the connotation of "edifying." Hymns and morality stories can be edifying, but critique connotes something very different. Professional critics insist, with good reason, that critique cannot be seen as valid only when it makes itself popular (and predictable!) through constructive suggestions. Whoever accepts critique only when it is advanced by someone who has a way to improve what is criticized—or at least claims to know how to improve it—is following a strategy of immunization. In the ongoing division of labor in modern bourgeois society, producer and critic have parted ways; as Hegel put it, one doesn't have to be a cobbler to know if the shoe fits. However, this perspective can turn into a complementary strategy of immunization. Criticism is in danger of making things too easy for itself if it loses sight of its normative premises. It must guard against that. A look at the function of criticism in the theoretical tradition to which Adorno belonged can help us grasp this dynamic.

Criticism is an essential element of thinking. When we reflect rationally on things—that is, when we think in a coherent and systematic way—then we are already behaving critically. To critique is to make distinctions and to decide rationally. "Critique" and "crisis" are connected not solely by their linguistic origins; rather, critique is crystallized in situations of crisis, as negation of the existing condition. However, the objective purpose of the negation is a better condition, something positive that ought to be generated, regardless of whether or how it is to be identified.

Since the Enlightenment, there has been much reflection on how the negative and positive sides of critique (or its destructive and constructive sides) are interconnected. The Enlightenment thinkers realized that critique is never an isolated undertaking, but always already a part of the philosophical process. Certainly, there are critics of art and literature, on the one hand, and philosophers, on the other, but the methodology and goals of critique are fundamentally philosophical. Hence Ernst Cassirer wrote of the "mental unity between philosophy and aesthetic literary criticism" in all the leading minds of the Enlightenment: "this unity is no accident with any of them; underlying it there is always a profound, inwardly necessary unity between the problems being confronted." Thus the Enlightenment saw the communion of philosophy and criticism as an "originary and substantial source of meaning." The Enlightenment "not only believes that philosophy and criticism are linked coherently in their indirect effects; it also asserts that they have a unitary essence, which it seeks to articulate."

The fact that, in the eighteenth century, critique became a key term for philosophy and aesthetics is linked to a social transformation. The emerging bourgeois society became a reality in the public sphere, where it set the tone. The urban way of life, with its salons and coffeehouses where aesthetic and political criticism were cultivated, played a decisive role. The bourgeoisie developed, in the context of the Enlightenment, the discursive forms appropriate to it, and took a critical stance toward prevailing social structures. In Germany, it was above all Kant who energized the Enlightenment impulse toward critique. Adorno agrees that Kant's critical philosophy "sought to emancipate society from its self-incurred immaturity" and that he "advocated autonomy, i.e., judgment on the basis of one's own insight, in opposition to heteronomy, namely, obedience to dicta imposed from without." As Herbert Schnädelbach explained it:

> For Kant the self-referentiality of reason underpins not only the systematizing of reason's accomplishments but also the critique of those accomplishments. Critique of rationality, that is, defining the limits of what it can achieve, is actually the self-critique of reason, as is indicated by the famous double meaning of the *Critique of Pure Reason*: critical and criticized reason are not distinct from each other. Thus ... for Kant capacity for critique is an essential marker of reason understanding itself. ... The self-critique of reason as a weapon against its own tendency to become blind and stupid, against its self-destruction and self-cancellation—this is surely the key legacy for today of Kant's concept of reason.

Part of Kant's legacy is that his concept of critique became socially consequential because he did not confine it to theoretical work. For Kant, critique is the task of the public realm. As the bourgeois society gradually developed, the public realm acquired a decisive function: it must initiate the learning process of the social collective that can turn that collective into a self-conscious agency of human self-determination. "Incorporated into the institutions of art criticism and criticism of literature, music, and theater, the judgment of a mature public (or one that views itself as mature) acquires a structure" (Habermas).

The same is true of political and philosophical discussion. As Jürgen Habermas argues, the bourgeois classes "constitute the public that long ago grew out of those early institutions of coffeehouse, salon, and dinner society, and is now held together by the mediation of the press and its professional criticism. They are the public face of a style of literary argument whereby the subjectivities of small family groupings reach a mutual understanding." To carry out the project of enlightenment, that is, to effect the emergence, at both the individual and the societal levels, "of humanity from its self-inflicted immaturity," requires the freedom "to make public use of reason in all contexts." This freedom has to be fought for and made secure, and criticism is indispensable to the process. Hence, Adorno contends, criticism is "essential to all democracy. Not only does democracy require the freedom to criticize and the impetus to do so; it is virtually defined by criticism. One can clarify this historically by noting that the separation of powers, a structure intrinsic to all democratic conceptions, from Locke through Montesquieu and the American constitution to the present, fundamentally lives through the critical process."

In the Enlightenment, therefore, it became clear that criticism's negative side is inseparable from its positive side. By seeking to destroy the untrue, the false, and the illusory, criticism aims to carry out the essential preliminary work for the construction of the true, the correct, and the essential. That is never a merely theoretical undertaking. Criticism, writes Marx, is not a passion of the mind but rather the mind of passion. On one side, there is the passionate struggle against social conditions that we cannot accept but must strive to transform. On the other side, there is the process of reflection that asks what is the essence of these conditions, what is their inner dynamic, and how they differ from genuinely humane conditions. Without understanding, the passionate effort to fight false and bad social relations just fizzles out. The reflecting power of reason is indispensable to the engagement of the heart.

The concept of critique, thus defined by the Enlightenment, was further developed by the critical theory of the nineteenth and twentieth centuries. Marx initially defines philosophy as "the ruthless critique of all social structures, ruthless both in the sense that critique does not flinch from its own results and in that it has no fear of the conflict with existing powers"; later he describes philosophy as the scientific "critique of political economy." As ruthless critic of all prevailing conditions, insofar as they cannot be justified by reason and the common goals of genuine human solidarity, Marx stands totally within the Enlightenment tradition. But by applying critique to the Enlightenment's own premises, he steps outside that tradition and becomes a radical critic of ideology. He demonstrates that the bourgeois public and its political institutions are based on economic assumptions that thwart the universal emancipatory claim underpinning Enlightenment critique.

At the center of bourgeois society stands the process of exploitation by capital. This process mandates the property owners' appropriation of the surplus produced by workers who, as wage earners, are a component of bourgeois society, but who at the same time drop out of it because, although they may freely own goods, they in fact own nothing but their labor, which they must sell in the marketplace. Hence, Habermas writes,

> the emancipation of bourgeois society from aristocratic rule does not lead to any neutralization of power in social relations between private citizens; instead, within the framework of free bourgeois contracts, new power relationships take shape, particularly those between property owners and wage laborers. This critical perspective ruptures all the fictions on which the ideal of civil society is based. . . . The society that Marx views himself as confronting contradicts its own principle of universal openness—the public can no longer claim to be identical with the nation, any more than bourgeois society can claim identity with society as such.

Critical theory in the twentieth century starts from these Marxian insights. In the 1930s, Horkheimer and the Institute for Social Research were intent on developing a conception of ideology-critique that would lay claim to the Enlightenment ideas of emancipation, autonomy, and responsibility, and, at the same time, explain why human beings, seemingly with free will, accept the return of old hierarchies. This conception includes the critique of the Soviet falsification of Marxist theory into an ideology legitimating authoritarian rule. Critical thinking in this sense aims to grasp the intricate involvement of reason in the overall processes of social self-reproduction. As in Marx's conception of critique, the method and the content of critical thinking are interwoven. Critical theory's goal is to change the social totality. To this end, its normative standard is its "interest in the revocation of social injustices." In this context, too, critique reflects on itself. For part of the process, it derives its norms from the situation under analysis. For Adorno, it is a first principle of critique that "it confronts realities with the norms to which those realities claim to subscribe; actually adhering to the norms would already be a better way." A society is thus measured by the extent to which it honors its objective claim to belong to everyone and makes a good life possible for all individuals according to their abilities.

"The attempt to legitimately define practical goals through critical thinking," as Horkheimer explains it in his seminal essay "Traditional and Critical Theory," foregrounds the concept of a future society as a community of free people, made possible by modern technologies. Adorno stresses that in nineteenth-century Germany, this idea of a better future society, enabled by critical thinking, was linked to the voluntary self-inspection of bourgeois modes of thought. The intellectual claim for emancipation on bourgeois terms, Adorno argues, is marked by contradictions. Philosophy tries to "silence" the critique it has itself unleashed—an attempt culminating in politically authoritarian "hostility to critique." Adorno sees a straight line from Hegel's law-based doctrine of the dominant state, according to which the "individual citizen should yield to reality," to the "denunciation" of the critic as a "divider" or, in Goebbels's phrase, a "caviler." The "German prejudice against criticism" leads Adorno back to social psychology and to the dangerous "identification with power," against which he fought continuously right through his last public writings.

3

Reason's Self-Criticism

WHOEVER COULD NOT OR WOULD NOT identify with the German state in 1933 had to leave if he valued his life. For many critical intellectuals driven out of Germany and Europe by fascism, emigration became a key experience in a double sense. In retrospect, it revealed the specific content of the social dynamics that had allowed the authoritarian state to emerge and had been absorbed in it. Moreover, expulsion provoked the mind to articulate *ex negativo* the outlines of a better life visible in the "damaged," alienated, thoroughly false life of that moment. The task was to recognize and conceptualize the individual's insignificance, his imprisonment by a rigid modern law of social relations that Weber had called a "steel casing" and which Marx had seen as structural alienation under the thumb of the "law of value." The signature element of modernity, which seemed to be endowed with a "natural" inevitability, had to be grasped and decoded without illusions, but was not to be accepted fatalistically. Socially critical theorists and artists formulated the seemingly paradoxical responsibility assigned by history to the experience of the vulnerable, endangered individual facing the threat of extinction.

"Truly I live in dark times!" wrote Bertolt Brecht, who had given Walter Benjamin refuge from the National Socialists, in his famous poem "To Posterity." The text reads:

> The innocent word is stupid. A smooth forehead
> Is a sign of insensitivity. He who laughs
> Has simply not yet heard
> The terrible news.
> What kind of times are these, when
> A conversation about trees is almost a crime,
> Because it entails silence about so many evil deeds?

Adorno's *Minima Moralia* contains an aphorism that seems like a theoretical comment on these lines, "Doctor, how nice of you." *Minima Moralia* not only contains highly sensitive, experientially based reflections on the changing face of social structures and everyday life; it also distills the central motifs of Adorno's philosophy and social theory. For this reason, the present introduction will return repeatedly to this work, which Adorno's subtitle labels "Reflections from Damaged Life."

"Doctor, how nice of you" reads as follows:

> Harmlessness no longer exists. The small pleasures, the expressions of life that appear exempt from the responsibility of thinking, not only contain an element of defiant stupidity, of obstinate blindness; they enter directly into the service of their extreme opposite. Even the blossoming tree connives in falsehood at the moment when its blossoming is experienced without the shadow of horror; even the innocent "how nice" becomes an escape from the shape of an existence that is quite the opposite.

The agonizing experience of the discrepancy between individual existence and defining social frameworks, drawn into tangible immediacy by the mass extermination of individuals, is given a vivid formulation by Adorno: even natural things, lacking both thought and subjectivity, must be judged according to the criteria of moral truth and falsity. In the total insanity of unfolding public events, not only objectified humans but even objects themselves are robbed of their right to exist, reduced to mere material for an alien project. The subject's objective claim to a rationally structured fusion of society and nature is transformed into absurdity by the irrationality of society—which, however, presents itself as second nature. In the mirror of objectivity, the objects of "first nature" now appear as liars because they seem to proclaim the utopia of successful living, of being for its own sake. But, according to Adorno, it is precisely from the pitiless insight that the possibility of a meaningful life is totally blocked that the power the subject needs in order to resist such a finality may grow: "there is no longer either beauty or consolation except in the gaze that approaches horror, confronts it and, in its irreducible awareness of the negative, holds firm to the possibility of a better world." That is the central motif underlying all of Adorno's theoretical and aesthetic writing: if the better world is conceivable at all, it is as the negation of the existent negativity. Adorno's theoretical and practical outlook, which has been termed, approvingly or disapprovingly, "negation," points always in a single direction: imagining, through specific negative insights, the overcoming of the prevailing negativity. Defined negation is the one perspective that can bring consolation to the endangered individual.

Defined Negation

This phrase alludes to a decisive starting point of Adorno's philosophy. "Defined negation" is a core category of Hegelian philosophy. One can call it Hegel's methodological principle, but to do so is problematic because it suggests the very separation of content and method that Hegel categorically rejected. For Hegel, all discussions of method must move *through* the content under discussion, not in isolation from it. Hegel sees dialectic as the intellectual expression of the real-life process being analyzed. Adorno made this perspective wholly his own.

The "idea," in Hegel's system, is always already self-contained at every stage of its historical movement. The idea therefore looks beyond its embodying moment, but for that reason is negatively bound to it. The immanent analysis of the historical moment is what Hegel terms "defined negation." Reflection on one's analysis, "thinking about thinking" (as Aristotle called it), is for Hegel inseparable from the reality of what is being analyzed: thinking is always simultaneously inside that reality. The core metaphysical and epistemological assumption of Hegelian idealism is that the individual entity, whether organic or conceptual, is constituted by negation, because it sets itself apart from the totality to which it belongs as a historical element. Thus it is tied by negation to the totality, and is then negated a second time when it imagines itself (or is imagined) as a part of that totality. The individual being is reunited with the larger whole, from which it first had to detach itself in order to achieve self-consciousness; the process of defining individual thought becomes a component of a systematic intellectual construction.

According to Hegel, totality—the absolute—is crystallized in this negative process. And all its individual moments, that is, everything that has been relativized returns, comprehended, to the entirety from which it originally emerged—but only in order to pull away again immediately. For Hegel, negating the negation becomes both the driving force of world history and the motivating law of logical thought processes. It becomes something positive. As he sees it, everything is defined by the negativity that inheres in it—by the fact that it becomes what it is only by relating negatively to everything that it is not. The contradiction, the confluence of conflicting negativities, becomes the movement of negating negation and thus propels world history.

However, Hegel characterizes "defined negation," the philosophical sublimation of this negative movement, as positive, because in the process of negating negation, defined negation "sublimates itself. . . . This self-referentiality is affirmation as such." Universal negativity, in its role as absolute law of mediation, has been transformed by idealism's magic wand into an affirmative principle.

Hegel's absolute idealism recognizes the essence of thinking with unsurpassed accuracy:

> By thinking of an object I turn it into a thought and cancel its sensuous being; I turn it into something that is essentially and without mediation my own: for only in thought am I wholly myself, only in the conceptual act do I penetrate the object that ceases to be apart from me and from which I have taken the essence that had separated it from

me. As Adam tells Eve, you are flesh of my flesh, bone of my bone—so the spirit says: this is spirit of my spirit, otherness has disappeared. Every mental image is a generalization that belongs to the process of thinking. To generalize something means to think it.

Mediation between the general and the particular is for Hegel a specific form of defined negation. He presupposes that what constitutes the principle of thought is also the principle of being. This idealist sleight of hand is the basis of the assumption that thinking defines being. The assumption makes sense given the premise that being is itself idea, thinking in its essence. In fact, Hegel simply articulates the principle of thinking. But in doing so he demonstrates that human social relations—which include nature insofar as it stands in relation to us—are constituted to some extent by reason.

Without abandoning this insight, Marx, the philosophical founder of nineteenth-century critical theory, himself "definitely negated" Hegel's intellectual image of defined negation. He sought, on the one hand, to demonstrate its ultimate untruth and, on the other, to adapt the element of truth it did contain to his own thinking. The core elements of Adorno's critique of idealism are already present in the work of the young Marx. This becomes especially clear when Marx criticizes Hegel's political philosophy in explicit detail. He takes seriously Hegel's claim of watching only the movement of the objects of thought, that is, of reproducing them in accordance with their own essential nature. Marx demonstrates that Hegel cannot do justice to this claim because his speculative construction of political reality actually dissolves reality, and what genuinely determines it, into the determinations of thought. Marx follows Feuerbach's materialist "critique of speculative philosophy," which claims to unmask that philosophy's practice of switching the roles of subject and predicate. That is to say, what appears in Hegel's philosophy to be the active principle, the subject, is in fact an installation as absolute of what should be seen as derived from, as attributed to, a predicate of the actual subject. At the end of the medieval era, nominalism sought to show that there were no autonomous, universal essences that, as metaphysical principles, lent their being to individual, concretely existing things. In the same way, Feuerbach seeks to demystify Hegel's hypostasizing of the idea. He endeavors to destroy the illusion that there is such a thing as a substantial, autonomous idea that, as the subject of the historical process, underlies all phenomena.

With Marx, the critique of the confusion between logic and ontology is politically intensified. For him, Hegel's philosophy does not pursue the logic inherent in the facts, but rather develops the logic of thought determinations in order to clothe the facts in it. Marx argues that because Hegel presents the autonomous development of the idea as the autonomous development of history's facts, he disables objectivity, that is, political reality, thus transforming it into a sequence of incidental expressions of the idea in its self-propulsion. Marx analyzes Hegel's attempt, in the core argument of the *Philosophy of Right*, to demonstrate with logical categories the mediation of particular and general interests in the state, thereby rendering the state "logically necessary." Using microanalysis, Marx shows how Hegel confuses thought patterns that emerge from the real, historical-social-(re)productive processes of human living with substantive, autonomous forces. The idea is mystified and fetishized as a Being both self-contained and forcefully affecting the world. Logical categories acquire agency; concrete content is dissolved into form. Conceptual definitions of the state are not analyzed but are treated as metaphysical, self-generating definitions. Marx writes, "Philosophy should investigate not how thought is embodied in political categories, but how existing political categories are dissolved into abstractions. The philosophical element is not the logic of the situation, but the situatedness of logic. Logic does not demonstrate the validity of the state; rather, the state is necessarily subject to the validation of logic ... thus the entire *Philosophy of Right* is but a parenthesis to the centrality of logic."

Adorno actualized this thinking at a historical moment when it had become obvious to him that both Hegel's social model and Marx's socialist certainty were obsolete. Hegel's presumption in favor of totality needing to construct itself by means of contradictions both spiritual and material, Adorno argued, led to a systemically necessary subordination of the individual to the social whole. "The fact that in prehistory the 'objective' tendency prevails without reference to individuals, indeed by means of their destruction, and that to this day the conceptually constructed reconciliation of the general and the particular has not established itself in practice: this core reality is distorted" in Hegel's thinking. "With cool superciliousness he opts once again for the liquidation of the particular. At no point does he question the primacy of the general."

In his three studies of Hegel, Adorno credits Hegel's perspective with the fundamental abolition of the fiction of individual autonomy, a fiction still nourished by Enlightenment philosophy, above all by Kant. Yet Hegel, in Adorno's view, shatters this fiction for the wrong reason. He does it not to demonstrate that the urgently needed autonomy of the individual is not yet realized, but expressly to point out that we should liberate ourselves from the conceptual structuring of a socially actualized autonomy of all individuals, of the a priori right of the individual in relation to the "supremacy of the general," because that is nothing but an empty utopia.

But so long as the promise of the reconciliation of free individual self-determination with social totality is not redeemed—and only human solidarity could achieve this—we continue to live, so Marx and Adorno both claim, in "prehistory." Marx assumes that bourgeois social formation represented the final stage of that prehistory, because it already contained the basic elements of a genuinely human history and was initiating the process of species emancipation. For Marx, the "bourgeois relations of production" were "the final antagonistic form of the production of society, antagonistic not in the sense of a conscious individual attitude, but rather of an antagonism growing out of individuals' lived social conditions." But for Marx there is another core truth: "the productive forces developing at the center of bourgeois society simultaneously create the material conditions for the resolution of this antagonism. Hence this social formation concludes the prehistory of human society."

The critical theory of the twentieth century does not share Marx's certainty. For Adorno, this prehistory is being perpetuated into an unforeseeable future, even while bourgeois society has been decisively transformed. "Objective tendency," "objective powers": those are the terms Adorno uses for a postfascist society defined entirely by the profit-oriented process of commodity production. For Adorno, today's society is ruled by a production process that has become autonomous in the social era in which we still live; that systematically masks its humane potential; and that, as a totality without subjectivity, degrades to mere appendages the human beings whose subsistence it supposedly nourishes and for whose sake it supposedly operates. As Adorno puts it in *Negative Dialectics*, "The experience of that objectivity, preprogrammed into the individual's consciousness, is the experience of the unity of the totally socialized society." In this, Adorno recognizes Hegel's "philosophical idea of absolute identity," realized in a distorting mirror. He concurs with Marx that identity, historical totality is actualized in the form not of logical contradictions but of thoroughly material and painful social antagonisms. He thus inverts Hegel's famous dictum from *The Phenomenology of Spirit*: Hegel asserts, as a definition of the universal, "The totality is truth. But the totality only attains its being in the process of its temporal unfolding." Adorno, whose concern is purely for the social whole, counters, "The totality is untruth."

The concept of totality is indispensable to critical theory, which could not conceptualize its theme—society as such—without this concept. In that sense, Adorno's thinking is tied to Hegel's. But critical theory's perspective on totality presupposes the goal of overturning, in practice, the existent totality. Only in this perspective does the recognizable essence of the false social whole reveal itself as untruth. To that extent, Adorno follows the emancipatory and revolutionary argument of Marxism. For Marx, defined negation meant not only theoretical critique but also, above all, practical critique. Marx opposes idealist philosophy on the basis of its own historical and social premises. For Marx, idealist negation is itself negated by the practical "imperative to overturn all social relations in which the individual is a humiliated, enslaved, abandoned, despised being." But in *Minima Moralia* Adorno, echoing Horkheimer's terminology, categorizes the philosophies of Hegel and Marx as "traditional theory" and "critical theory"; for him the perspective of metaphysical or historical reconciliation is no longer available. For Marx, the moment seemed to have arrived when the possibility of fulfilling philosophy's unsettled claims through revolutionary praxis could be realized. For Adorno, this possibility of social actualization is today indefinitely blocked. In his view, the epochal opportunity to establish a free society—in which the promises of freedom and autonomy articulated by nineteenth-century idealist and materialist philosophies would be fulfilled—was squandered. The failed project of a Soviet republic, followed, after a brief democratic interlude, by the authoritarian state that drove into exile the critical intellectuals, the legitimate heirs of the great German philosophers—for Adorno this was the political turning point.

The Two Faces of Enlightenment

While Adorno was writing *Minima Moralia*, he was working with Max Horkheimer on their seminal philosophical study of critical theory, *Dialectic of Enlightenment*. This book marks the transition from the collective undertaking of the Institute for Social Research to the philosophical work of individuals, which took place in the 1940s. It embodies a reaction to the transformed social and historical circumstances of that time. In light of the triumph of fascism, which, in these authors' eyes, the rest of the world countered only with a complementary tendency toward political and economic totalitarianism, Adorno and Horkheimer saw little promise in the project of using an interdisciplinary materialist theory to effect revolutionary change. Rather, according to *Dialectic of Enlightenment*, it is time to understand "why humanity, rather than entering a truly human condition, is sinking into a new kind of barbarism." To explain this, the book begins with the dialectical thesis that myth and modern rationality are intertwined.

Siegfried Kracauer had already formulated this idea in 1927 in his essay "The Ornament of the Masses." In his brilliant investigation of the aesthetic forms of modern mass culture, such as the figurations of the Tiller girls who danced in Berlin during the inflation years, structural relations are constructed between the surface manifestations of popular culture and its social base, relations to be understood via the philosophy of history. Kracauer interprets the dialectic of reason and nature—a dialectic between the rational core of mythology and the mythological element in rationality—as an unchanging background against which the unresolved conflicts of human prehistory, defined by alien forces, return, compulsive and unfinished, in the most modern manifestations of social existence: "History is inaugurated by a weak, distant version of reason, fighting against the powers of nature that, in mythology, ruled heaven and earth. After the twilight of the gods, the gods did not abdicate; primal nature asserts itself within and around human beings." But this primal nature asserts itself without concepts. In the organicist social theory of the conservatives and the communitarian illusion of the populists, unreconciled nature asserts itself in a false form. But the situation is basically no better with the opposite politics, with "the project of enlightenment," as it would be called today. Its progressive rationality has in no way achieved harmony with itself. Kracauer demonstrates this by analyzing the wholly rational and constructed products of the economic sector newly prominent in the 1920s: mass culture. He describes mass culture's contradictory identity. Its formally rational surface is derived from its Taylorist, decentered structure, from the division of labor; it is composed of meaningless, individual segments that are actually human beings. Their nature, their individual qualities, and their needs are all irrelevant. "The ornament of the masses is the aesthetic reflection of the rationality sought by the prevailing economic system," Kracauer writes.

> The capitalist era is a stage on the path to demystification. The way of thinking structured into today's economic system has made possible a domination and exploitation of nature unthinkable in earlier times.... Yet the rationality of capitalist economics is not reason itself, but a clouded form of reason. At a particular point it abandons the category of truth, in which it is engaged. It does not include the individual. The course of the production process is not organized with any regard for individuals; the economic and social system is not based on them; and at no point is the foundation of the human identical with the foundation of the system. I repeat: the foundation of the human. For the point is not that capitalist thinking should treat individuals as historically developed entities, that it should leave their personalities intact and focus on satisfying their corporeal needs. Those who think this way

charge capitalism with violating individuals by means of its remorseless rationality, and yearn for the renewed emergence of a community that supposedly embodies the essentially human better than capitalist society. [But those critics] . . . fundamentally miss the core affliction of capitalism. It is not too rational, but not rational enough. The style of thinking it imposes resists the perfectibility of reason that speaks from the foundation of the human.[1]

In *Dialectic of Enlightenment*, Adorno and Horkheimer no longer talk of "the human." Their way of arguing, unlike Kracauer's, is no longer defined methodologically by the fusion of critical Marxism with phenomenology and life philosophy.[2] At the same time, the fundamental motif of their dialectic, the interweaving of reason with myth, refers back to Kracauer, who sums it up thus: "If the ornament of the masses is viewed from the perspective of reason it is revealed as a mythological cult concealed in abstract clothing." The ornaments that fascism offered the masses a little later can accordingly be read as an abstract cult, that is, an external cult not based on faith but shrouded in a mythological robe.

Other important sources of inspiration for *Dialectic of Enlightenment* include motifs of Walter Benjamin's philosophy contained in his book of aphorisms, *One-Way Street* (1928), and the "Theses on the Philosophy of History" (1940). In *One-Way Street*, Benjamin decodes the double rhythm in the behavior of children—the return of humanity's animistic magical eras and the gradual transition to orientation by purpose-driven rationality—as an intertwining of mythological and enlightened thinking. Enchantment and disenchantment of the world are inseparable, and this intertwining has both good and bad outcomes. Children who find hiding places in their homes nestle up mimetically against objects, thereby learning to control them:

> The child standing behind the curtain himself becomes something flowing and white, a kind of ghost. The dining-room table, under which he crouches, is imagined as the wooden idol of a temple, with its carved legs as the four pillars. And hiding behind a door the child is himself a door, claiming a role as its severe mask, as a magician ready to bewitch all who unsuspectingly enter. . . . In this way the home is an

arsenal of masks. Yet once a year gifts appear in its secret places, in its empty eye sockets, its rigid mouth. Experiencing it magically becomes a science. As engineer of his parents' gloomy dwelling, the child demystifies it and hunts down Easter eggs.

Still more important for the dialectic of enlightenment is the apocalyptic perspective from which Benjamin views history in his final work, the "Theses on the Philosophy of History." In the ninth thesis, Benjamin is inspired by Paul Klee's print "Angelus Novus" to construct an allegory of the "angel of history." In this angel's perspective from the beyond, the entirety of human history, which appears to us as "a chain of events," looks like "a single catastrophe, ceaselessly piling wreckage upon wreckage and hurling it at the angel's feet. He wishes he could linger, awaken the dead, and repair what is shattered. But a storm blows from paradise, becoming entangled in his wings, and is so powerful that the angel can no longer close them. This storm propels him ceaselessly into the future, to which he turns his back, while the pile of wreckage facing him grows ever higher. This storm is what we call progress." Benjamin lodges a vehement protest against the Second International's universalist and progressive faith in history; his thesis is that a conceptually faithful revolution would have to "shatter the continuum of history," not to fulfill history. "A critique of the idea of progress," from the perspective of the defeated, "the oppressed, . . . teaches us," Benjamin claims with regard to fascism's destruction of all revolutionary tendencies, "that the 'exceptional condition' in which we live is actually the rule. . . . The amazement that what we're experiencing is 'still' possible in the twentieth century is not a philosophical perspective. It will not lead to any insight—except the truth that the conception of history from which it derives is unsustainable." Thus the perspective from which history is to be reconstructed must be negative.

The authors of *Dialectic of Enlightenment* transpose Benjamin's negative philosophy of history into the field of the critique of reason. The twentieth century has realized the goals of the Enlightenment: rationality and science have been comprehensively developed. Earlier mythological attempts to dominate nature and enable self-determination for human beings—for Horkheimer and Adorno the historical prototypes of enlightenment—have been triumphantly replaced by technology and industry. Progressive rationality destroys the certainties of mythological cosmology. Adorno and Horkheimer describe the ongoing process of reducing reason to formulae as a permanent twilight of the idols, which finally, under the rule of the "ratio of capital,"[3] culminates in the death of God—but only in order to replace the demystified prerational ideals with the false idolatry of a formalized, scientifically truncated version of reason. In the victory march of the Enlightenment, Horkheimer and Adorno perceive the Enlightenment's antithesis. Reason becomes the tool of domination. Scientific rationality becomes a rigid, closed system to which everything is subsumed, whether it fits or not. The most highly developed condition of modern productive forces serves the highest imaginable degree of destruction, namely, war and the industrially organized mass murder of human beings. In this critical sense, enlightenment has not been realized—or, as Horkheimer and Adorno formulate it, "Enlightenment reverts to mythology."

This process of enlightenment's self-destruction is to be countered by its "self-contemplation." The authors do not abandon reason, do not invoke some "other" as a remedy for it. They resist the "fashionable ideology that dedicates itself to the liquidation of enlightenment." They thereby draw an unmistakable line between themselves and the reactionary critique of enlightened civilization advanced by Oswald Spengler, Ludwig Klages, and Rudolf Borchardt—even as they nevertheless owe something to these theorists' indictment of modernity. However, Horkheimer and Adorno do not formulate a theory of enlightenment's decadence. They articulate the "double meaning" of enlightenment, which, as a "core historical phenomenon," they ascribe not only to a particular historical intellectual era but also to the concept of enlightenment as such; following Nietzsche, they include all "progressive" thinking in this category. Hence their investigation is extended "to the beginning of recorded history."

Dialectic of Enlightenment contains five chapters and a collection of aphorisms. First, a dialectical "concept of enlightenment" is developed. In the subsequent "excursus," Adorno reconstructs the genesis of modern subjectivity through a reading of the *Odyssey*. Its wandering hero, who cunningly holds onto life, is interpreted as "the primal image ... of the bourgeois individual ... the concept of which is rooted in that unitary self-assertion so vividly exuded by the prehistoric wanderer." Adorno intends to show that the autonomy of the subject, the core motif of the Enlightenment, is already inscribed in the emergence of the epic from myth, in a dialectical form of which the epic hero is not himself conscious. In the second excursus, Horkheimer explores the link between enlightenment and moral philosophy. As he sees it, bourgeois thinking has as its ideal the seamless systematicity of scientific reason, which is not in itself capable of rationally justifying moral intuitions and hence can only generate impotent moralizing proclamations. In contrast to bourgeois thinking, the darkly "immoralist" middle-class authors Sade and Nietzsche had the merit of "not attempting, like the apologists of Enlightenment, to evade its consequences through pseudoharmonizing doctrines. . . . They did not pretend that formalist reason stood in a closer relation to morality than to immorality. While the intelligentsia protected, through a process of denial, the ongoing linkage between reason and immoral acts, between bourgeois society and domination, Sade and Nietzsche gave uncompromising voice to the shocking truth."

In the chapter "Culture Industry," Adorno argues that the "eternal return of the same" (as Nietzsche put it), a core element of myth, is also the principle of twentieth-century mass culture, generating products at the highest technical level and keeping consumers in thrall to a constant need to replace them. And in the final chapter, "Elements of Anti-Semitism," both authors, working with Leo Löwenthal, analyze the failure of enlightenment as the historical unfolding of the quest for rationality. The chapter combines social-psychological and economic elements with a concept of mimetic behavior that became indispensable to critical theory. The fascist agitator imitates the hated, supposedly Jewish attitudes and behaviors of the victims in order to launch the pogrom, whereby the perpetrators can regressively act out their violent, archaic impulses. But the agitator's ploys and the pogrom structured by science and technology are highly rational undertakings. The mimetic impulse, which belongs to early human developmental phases, is enlisted in the service of authoritarian rule in order to make individuals' regressive needs useful for the perpetuation of power. Civilization makes use of regression and retreat from civilization in order to maintain itself, thereby unmasking its success as failure. *Dialectic of Enlightenment* concludes with a collection of Horkheimer's aphorisms, restaging in a compressed form the book's critical and anthropological themes.

The text was published as a duplicated typescript in 1944 by the Institute for Social Research under the title *Philosophical Fragments* (which later became the book's subtitle). Then, in 1947, it was published as a book under the title *Dialectic of Enlightenment* by Querido Verlag, Amsterdam. A subterranean influence emanated from the book; Adorno frequently mentioned that he saw all his later major writings as excursuses to *Dialectic of Enlightenment*. But the volume was not published in the Federal Republic; anyone in the know could readily obtain a copy from Amsterdam, but few people did so. During the student movement in the 1960s, printed editions circulated, both of the book and of Horkheimer's printed essays from the *Journal of Social Research*. Horkheimer could no longer resist the urgent demand for a new edition of *Dialectic of Enlightenment*, a project to which, even earlier, Adorno had not objected. In 1969 it appeared in an edition published by S. Fischer Verlag.

Irving Wohlfarth made the critical point that Horkheimer and Adorno themselves adopt the perspective of Benjamin's "angel of history." From this point of view, no doubt, derives the curiously predictable character of the dialectic of enlightenment, as evoked by Detlev Claussen: "the false impression that everything is already decided in the embryo." Yet this dialectical aporia is productive, for it enables the articulation of a pointedly critical theory of the historical process—which was Horkheimer's goal from the outset. In order to explain fascism as the current form of violent domination over both nature and human beings, *Dialectic of Enlightenment*, in the opinion of Christoph Türcke and Gerhard Bolte, elaborates a "deepening of the Marxist concept of prehistory." This deepening is also important for understanding the way Adorno uses the concept of prehistory in *Minima Moralia*. As he writes in the 1960s, "What Marx, with a kind of melancholy hopefulness, calls prehistory is quite simply the essence of all known history to this point, the empire of unfreedom." Wherein lies the "deepening" of the concept projected by *Dialectic of Enlightenment*? Türcke and Bolte write:

> Insofar as Horkheimer and Adorno take literally the notion of capitalism as the most advanced stage of prehistory, they are able to focus on the prehistory of capitalism itself. It both is prehistory and has prehistory, and one understands it fundamentally only when one grasps the prehistory contained within it and reads prehistory's structure out of actually existing capitalist structures, thereby reaching the deep structure of prehistory as such. Only in this way, as Horkheimer and Adorno see it, can one achieve an understanding of the horrors of fascism: in fascism is expressed not only capitalism but the whole violent mythical power of prehistory, which fascism absorbed and endowed with maximum technological capacities.[4]

In this way, a totalizing perspective is adopted that strengthens the philosophical orientation of critical theory—an orientation that was unmistakably present from the outset in Horkheimer's studies defining the methodological practice of the Institute for Social Research. For *Dialectic of Enlightenment* is not concerned only with fascism. The opposing system, Stalinism, is analyzed, but not in a simplistic or demagogic way as fascism's double. Horkheimer and Adorno outline a theory of the "totalitarian state,"[5] starting from its social manifestations but focused on an understanding of the structure of totality. In other words, they use a critical concept of totality as a basis, without which—as was shown with regard to Adorno's concept of the whole—no structural insight is possible, and hence no critique of totalitarianism. But the critical concept of totality cannot be derived from empirical knowledge. It is directed at the foundational principle of sociopolitical phenomena, a principle that does not appear as such and hence is a kind of placeholder for unfinished metaphysical analysis in a postmetaphysical age.

4

Rescuing What is Beyond Hope

EVEN AFTER HIS RETURN FROM EXILE, it remained important for Adorno to keep working on the key problems of philosophy. "Philosophy, which at one point seemed outdated, stays alive because the moment of its realization was missed": this he wrote in *Negative Dialectics* concerning the young Marx, who had spoken of the sublimation of philosophy through its realization within the social whole.

Philosophy from the Perspective of Redemption

But what should philosophy look like in the present? Its program is already sketched out in *Minima Moralia*. In the final aphorism, titled "In Conclusion," Adorno writes,

> The only way to justify philosophy in the face of despair would be the attempt to observe all things as they would appear from the perspective of redemption. Knowledge has no light but that which shines from

redemption onto the world: everything else is used up in the attempt to construct meaning after the fact, the effort remains fragmentary. Perspectives need to be generated in which the world distends and alienates itself, reveals its rifts and cracks in exactly the way it will one day appear, needy and disfigured, in the light of the Last Judgment.

Adorno here adopts Walter Benjamin's motif of messianic theology—whose secularized truth content reaches fulfillment in historical materialism—and situates it in the context of a programmatic reflection on his own striving for philosophical knowledge. Benjamin described the role of theology in his speculative materialist philosophy as follows: "My thinking relates to theology as blotting paper to ink. It is completely saturated by it. But if it were up to the blotting paper, nothing that is written would survive."

Adorno's philosophical move is to adopt the perspective of redemption, which, theologically, no longer has credibility. He therefore has no actual expectation of redemption. Adorno borrows from the radical theological perspective that refuses to align itself to what actually exists, always seeking transcendence; yet he does not rely on the intervention of messianic transcendence to bring about a redemption not of this world. When Benjamin declares that "redemption is the limit of progress," he is speaking of the worldly boundary that stands in the way of the elimination of suffering and the establishment of a truly humane world. This perspective is based on the observation that, on the one hand, the humane goal seems to have become totally unreachable and, on the other, even a fully rational society could no longer mitigate the irrevocable sufferings of the past. On this point, Rolf Tiedemann describes the relation between Adorno and Benjamin as follows:

> In view of the breakdown of enlightenment and civilization, particularly of the clear possibility of a definitive catastrophe, it makes sense to give up the thought of progress in favor of a transcendental intervention, a rupture of history; Benjamin inclined to this view. But not Adorno: in such messianism he discerned a "flight into ahistorical theology" that had to be resisted. He insisted that the emphatic social ideals that once inspired hope are interwoven in the historical

process—and that this process, with its enduring blindness and growing irrationality, requires one to reflect on the transcendental telos of those ideals, encoded in their theological names. It is for the sake of immanence that Adorno allows himself the thought of transcendence, for the sake of the empirical world that he refuses to let go the idea of the absolute. Materialism is the essential content of that "radicalization of dialectics to its passionate theological core" which Adorno demanded of Benjamin, and which he understood as his own mission.

Already, in the 1930s, Adorno termed "the salvation of the hopeless" as the "core element" of his theoretical work; in the final aphorism of *Minima Moralia* he pursues the problem of how a philosophy should proceed that could help give expression to what is transitory and threatened, thereby conceptualizing the world's need of redemption. He formulates his solution as an aporia:

> The whole purpose of thinking is to achieve such perspectives without arbitrariness and intellectual violence, solely through empathy with objects. It is very simple, because the state of things cries out for such recognition, indeed because radical negativity, once clearly confronted, becomes, in a flash, the mirror image of its opposite. But it is also quite impossible, because it presupposes a perspective that is removed from the influence of existence, even if just by a tiny bit—whereas in actuality any potential insight must not only be wrested from what exists in order to become binding, but must in the process be pounded by the very same distortion and neediness it proposes to escape.

Hegel's "pure contemplation" is placed in the service of both individual objects in need of redemption and the awful totality: nothing is more straightforward than describing what *is* while compellingly demonstrating that mere description does not fulfill the task, that the actual must be changed. The pure immanence of immersion in the objects of knowledge brings to light the negative image of that which would surpass the immanence of what is. As Adorno formulates the issue in *Negative Dialectics*, "Only if what is can be changed, is the existent world not the totality." Yet this simple task is simultaneously insoluble, because the philosopher himself is also immersed in the very "context of blindness" that he proposes to grasp and penetrate. The conceptual fluidity between immanence and transcendence makes it impossible to define the standpoint from which the critical subject views the world and to situate that standpoint in a clear relation to the object of critique.

Adorno himself was the first to thematize what later interpreters of his work point to as the cardinal defect of his radicalization of the critique of ideology: namely, that he did not prove his critical perspective to be free of contradictions. Adorno saw that the only philosophy capable of advancement is the one that acknowledges this aporia, and he saw clearly the consequences of taking this conceptual claim seriously: "Nothing less is demanded of today's thinker than that he locate himself at every moment both inside and outside the empirical world: the gesture of Münchhausen [the eighteenth-century teller of tall war stories], who pulls himself by the hair out of the swamp, is central to every insight that claims to be more than either factual assertion or intellectual projection. And then the tenured philosophers come along and make the objection that we have no firm point of view." Adorno simply did not believe that the perspective of the critical philosopher elevated him above the totality on which his critique is focused. He is locked into it, but it would be false to insist that radical critique must either develop a clear point of view outside its object of critique or else fall silent. Critique derives its criteria not from some foundational truth actualized either existentially or by decisive argumentation, but from its object of critique, and when this object is the very process of philosophical thinking, then critique turns on itself and analyzes its own methodologies. In this way, reason's philosophical self-critique stands in a disrupted yet productive relation to the tradition. Critical thinking embodies participation in the philosophical self-analysis mediated by tradition and in its material assumptions. As was already clear to Marx, critique must decisively negate both. As Adorno puts it in *Negative Dialectics*, "Tradition is immanent to any insight . . . as the mediating vehicle of its analytical objects."

The question then arises for Adorno of "how thinking that must renounce tradition could preserve it in the very gesture of transformation." Hermeneutically, this process cannot be smooth. The aporia linking the radical critique of reason to a philosophical commitment to the individual, specific, and ephemeral cannot be overcome by dialectical reflection on the relationship to tradition. On the contrary: one must acknowledge this aporia in order to do justice to its force. Adorno continues in the final aphorism of *Minima Moralia*: "the more passionately thought seals itself off from what has conditioned it—for the sake of unconditioned goals—the more unconsciously, hence fatefully, it succumbs to the empirical world. For the sake of the possible, thought must even grasp its own impossibility. In the face of the demand thought thereby makes upon itself, even the question of the reality or unreality of redemption becomes almost a matter of indifference." What is needed is thinking that incorporates its own aporias into the process of self-reflection.

Primacy of the Object

"Reflection on thinking's own aporias": that is the agenda of Adorno's *Negative Dialectics*. Negative dialectics is simply the defined negation of idealist dialectics. Its goal is to liberate the specific, the nonidentical, from subordination to conceptual identity and generality. Negative dialectics becomes central to Adorno's philosophy; it incorporates both elements of his early philosophical work on Edmund Husserl's phenomenology and the self-critique of rationality that is expounded in *Dialectic of Enlightenment.*

In *Negative Dialectics*, Adorno aims to critique what he terms "philosophy of the origin." The negative dialectician Hegel's speculative dialectics is the systemic and historical climax of metaphysics. Since its origin, the goal of metaphysics has been to structure a firm ground of being, which could then serve as a basis from which thinking could derive principles, accessible through reason, that would render coherent the seemingly chaotic variety of actually existing objects. The reductionism that makes reason into the origin of that which may participate in reason—but which for that very reason cannot be identical with reason, cannot be dissolved into it without a significant residue—this reductionism, viewed from the perspective of a materialist reconstruction of intellectual and cultural history, simply had to be viewed as outdated. "Domination of nature" is thus, for Adorno, " the basis of philosophical idealism."

Human beings can only orient themselves—that is, structure and control a world that initially appears as an irresistible set of natural forces—when they are able to impose systematicity on what overwhelms them, seeming to flood in unpredictably. This systematicity derives exclusively from the logical mechanism underpinning our rational processes. Ancient philosophy endowed it with timeless validity in the shape of logical axioms, whose utmost imperative was to avoid contradiction. Thus Aristotle writes,

> It is clearly the task of the philosopher, and whoever studies the nature of all beings, to analyze the principles of reasoning. It is, however, appropriate that the person who knows the most about a particular field is the one to provide the most well-tested principles for judging it; hence the person with the fullest knowledge of being, as it is manifest in the world, can provide the surest principles for defining it. That person is the philosopher. But the most secure of all principles is the one that precludes error. This principle must be instantly recognizable and without preconditions. . . . We can now assert what that principle is; for it is impossible that the same quality should be both present and not present in the same object in the same context. . . . That is therefore the most secure principle of all.

Without the laws of thinking, which we are always already applying even before we are conscious of them, there would be no knowledge. Adorno does not disagree with this principle, notwithstanding his irrational admirers and rationalist critics—both groups that would like to make him into a harbinger of postmodernity. Adorno wants to show, rather, that knowledge deserving of the name is more than rule-bound subordination of sensuous and intellectual material under logical systematicity. More precisely, he takes a step further: knowledge in this restricted sense is always only knowledge of self. Not self-knowledge in the enlightening sense invoked by classical antiquity when it formulated "Know thyself!" as the radical telos of philosophy, or when it enabled Oedipus to solve the Sphinx's riddle through human self-awareness, but in the sense of a confusion. This type of knowledge puts forward as substantial experience of objectivity that which is in fact only the subject's self-mirroring. The insights into the order of things that reason gains on this narrow path are attributed to the world's actuality in its very own, most inward essence.

As Adorno puts it, following Nietzsche, "Since Parmenides all ontology has been idealistic." Nietzsche, a pioneer of modernity's self-critique, recognized an inescapable aporia of metaphysics: the confusion of linguistically shaped thought patterns with definitions of being. In Nietzsche's view, the basis of idealist metaphysics is nothing but the violent story of the development and intensification of the subject. In *Dialectic of Enlightenment*, Adorno and Horkheimer decipher this story as the dialectic between the subject's domination of nature and its quasi-organic subordination to the rigidified institutions of domination.

As an enlightened dialectician, Nietzsche demystifies the fetish character of idealist *philosophia prima*. As he writes in *Twilight of the Idols*,

> We find ourselves enmeshed in a coarse fetishistic web when we try to summon up the basic premises of linguistic metaphysics, that is, in German, of reason [*Vernunft*]. Everywhere acts and actors are operative; there's a faith in the self, in the self as being, in the self as substance—and a projection onto all things of the faith in self-substance; only thus does the concept of "thing" become viable. . . . Being is conceptualized into everything as its cause; and yet the notion of "being" is itself a derivative of the conception of "self."

According to Nietzsche, the indispensable idealist trick that philosophy applies, without any intention to deceive, arises from

> the surprise with which the security, the subjective certainty in the deployment of categories of reason, entered the philosophers' consciousness. . . . They concluded that these categories could not be based in the empirical world—that world was wholly at odds with them. Then whence do they arise? In India, as in Greece, the same erroneous conclusion was drawn: "we must once have been at home in a higher world . . . we must have been divine—because we have Reason!"

Self-substance, which Nietzsche identifies as the silent operational premise underlying the projective mechanics of philosophy's thinking of objects, is expanded by Adorno into the core thematics of identity. For him, the confusion of rational categories with nonobjective reality amounts to an identity compulsion: the human mind cannot avoid classifying objects according to normalizing and deviant characteristics, according to the criteria of identity and nonidentity. Where this has not yet been achieved, there is no subject; where there is a prospect of overcoming it, the threat of the subject's disruption also comes into view. The classifying process, however, subsumes the diffuse, the exceptional, and the unique under a single cognitive schema. First, this schema must be able to prevail consistently as the subject's structure of knowing; second, it must dismantle the singularity of objects in order to classify them as categorized objects of knowledge compatible with the overall structures of our perceptions and concepts. This process unavoidably ruptures the actual identity of the objects of thought and subordinates them to the identity principle of the reasoning subject.

Identity thus has a double meaning, which Adorno deconstructs: it subsumes both the actual identity of the thing itself and the constructed identity, imposed from outside, of heterogeneous objects. The pressure toward identity is a mark of thinking as such; without it, thinking would be impossible. Yet this pressure is not exclusively a sign of reason but also an imprint of the very real external pressure to which all rational subjects are always subjugated, insofar as they, as individuals, belong to the totality of a society.

Adorno wants, by means of an immanent ideological critique of idealism, to shake open this seemingly indissoluble fusion of theoretical identity compulsion with the identity compulsion of social practice. Hegel, Marx, and Nietzsche are the starting points for his project to resurrect the "nonidentical." The purpose of this project is to demonstrate how idealism's identity compulsion misses the very goal it is aiming at, and to envision a kind of thinking that could do justice to a reality that does not merge seamlessly with thought: "the identity of mind with itself is projected methodologically onto its subject matter. . . . That is the original sin of *philosophia prima*.

Simply in order to ensure continuity and completeness, philosophy must expel everything that doesn't fit from the zone on which it is passing judgment." Tracing the history of philosophy from Parmenides and Plato through Descartes and Kant to the newly resurrected "originary" philosophy of Husserl's "contemplation of essence," with its goal of unlocking the "sphere of being of absolute origins"—or indeed to Heidegger's existential ontology—Adorno argues that philosophy's quest for first principles has always impelled it to uncover conceptual grounds for everything that is and to deduce from these grounds, in a clean and seamless methodological circle, the totality of what can be known. But in this process the knowing subject always recognizes only itself. Idealist metaphysics ossifies into the brilliant tautology of mind, because it cannot incorporate into knowledge anything that is alien from itself and which eludes identification with a general category. The tension between the particular and the general, or between the one and the many, is in actuality defused a priori, because all "devices for rendering the nonidentical commensurable with the subject under the name of the manifold" are constrained by "the model of unity." Thinking must operate within the framework of general definitions and hence subtract from objects of cognition any specific element that will not dissolve into the principle of unity. In modern philosophy, with Kant, idealism reaches a point where it demonstrates the inadequacy of the claim that philosophy should conceptually emulate the actually existing ideas, whence the variety of ephemeral individual objects arises. The concept of contemplative knowledge is replaced by the concept of knowledge as spontaneous constitution. Hume's empiricism demonstrated the unbridgeable distance between an objectivist metaphysics and individual cognitive subjects who, lacking any instrument of knowledge other than their senses, assemble their impressions associatively, according to habit. Against this critique, Kant proposes nevertheless to show the viability of metaphysics by demonstrating that the subject's world is not substantively independent of the subject. The subject constitutes objectivity, not randomly or individually, but following rules that are intrinsic to all subjects. These rules do not derive from experience, but enable us a priori to have experiences:

> The premise "I think" must accompany all my ideas. . . . The idea that can be said to precede all thinking . . . is an act of spontaneity. . . . I call it the originary apperception. . . . I also call its unity the transcendental unity of self-consciousness, in order to describe the a priori possibility of knowledge emerging from it. For the various ideas at work in a particular perspective would not, in their entirety, be my ideas if they did not, as an entirety, constitute a self-consciousness; that is, as my ideas they are necessarily subject to the conditioning whereby they are able to cohere in a general self-consciousness, since otherwise they would not be continually valid for me. . . . Thus the synthetic unity of apperception is the highest point at which one must integrate all uses of reason, indeed all logic, and, accordingly, transcendental philosophy. [Kant]

From the perspective of critical theory, Kant's argument is problematic. As Adorno's student and colleague Karl-Heinz Haag argues,

> The transcendental unity of apperception was not a content-based principle but an empty unity: a construction of the abstract philosophical process which hypostasized itself in the "highest point" of its activity. Philosophy reduced its own essence, which it fused with the identity of pure thinking, to its function: namely, the production of the necessary coherence of all phenomena.

On the side of the subject, Kant thereby saves the binding quality of norm-based knowledge, and with it the possibility of science, from the critique of empiricism. On the side of the object, his goal is to preserve from dissolution the objects of cognition, whose essence can no longer be dogmatically affirmed without lapsing into precritical metaphysics. To these ends, Kant constructs a distinction between the "thing in itself" and "appearance." "Apparent" nature is not independent of the perceptual principles governing the subject to whom it appears. Yet what appears is itself distinct from the process of appearing: it is the noumenon, "the unknown source of all appearances, which does not itself appear." In Kant's transcendental philosophy, the noumenon corresponds to what the metaphysical tradition termed "essence." Nature's laws are accessible to human beings only in conjunction with the laws of human perception. The transcendental subject is not passive, not merely receptive, but always actively participating in the production of the world that is the object of its cognition. But what that world is in itself, the totality of reality independent of spatiotemporal and causal laws, what defines its intelligible core in distinction from its empirical character—that is not positively knowable. Kant's philosophy thus eludes the traps of traditional metaphysics and is able to rehabilitate metaphysics as such. As Adorno puts it, fully in the Kantian spirit,

> Metaphysics, in its essence, consists not of clear dogmatic answers, but of questions. . . . Metaphysics cannot be identified with the doctrines of being that proclaim themselves to be metaphysical; for it consists precisely of the questions being addressed to such theories of being, without in any way prejudicing the real existence of these questions. To put it pointedly: negative metaphysics is just as metaphysical as the positive kind.

Following Adorno's lead, Karl-Heinz Haag later showed that this "negative metaphysics" is fundamental to Kant, because Kant knows that "nature's intelligible core cannot be positively defined" and that its "constitutive meaning for actually existing nature" can only be articulated by negation [Haag]. Yet Kant fails to reflect sufficiently on the social character of what it is that replaces the traditional version of being. That is the source of Kant's great ambiguity.

Adorno's critique of Kant productively advances this reflection. It can do so because it deliberately breaks the rules of an immanent philosophical reading of Kant. For Adorno, it is fundamental that the critique of knowledge cannot be separated from the critique of society. Thus the critique of idealism must thematize its unspoken social assumptions. According to Adorno, the most important of these assumptions is the absolute privileging of mental over physical work, pointing to the newly dominant social conditions of division of labor:

> The general and necessary activity of the mind is grounded in unavoidable social labor. . . . The a priori concept of the transcendental subject, a nonbeing that is nevertheless active; of something general that yet experiences the particular—this premise resembles a soap bubble that could never be derived from the context of autonomous

immanence that shapes each necessarily individual consciousness.... Outside the magic circle of the philosophy of identity, the transcendental subject can be decoded as the social base that is not aware of itself as such.... The qualities that, since the *Critique of Pure Reason*, have defined the transcendental subject—functionality, pure activity that expresses itself in the accomplishments of individuals while simultaneously transcending them—these qualities are projected, by the intellect in its bubble, onto the pure subject of their source.... Yet the general nature of the transcendental subject is that of the functional context of society, of a totality constituted by individual spontaneities and qualities, which are then contained by means of the leveling exchange principle—and then virtually excluded as being impotently dependent on the totality. The universal dominance of exchange value over human beings, denying subjects a priori the status of being subjects, then reducing subjectivity to the status of impotent object—this dominance relegates to the status of untruth the general principle claiming to establish the primacy of the subject.

In *Negative Dialectics*, Adorno affirms the epistemological premise of the "primacy of the object." He stresses that, of all the idealist philosophers, Kant does the greatest justice to the object. Adorno does not want to deny that, epistemologically speaking, objects are knowable only through the subjectivity that mirrors them. At the same time, he disputes Kant's reduction of objects to the status of being defined entirely by the autonomous subject. In Kant's work, as Adorno sees it, autonomous thinking becomes conscious of its own strength and shakes off the ontological fetters of traditional metaphysics by reflecting on itself and its constitutive function. But that is also the point at which thinking is transformed into its own fetishization: into subjective reason. According to Horkheimer, subjective reason implies "the capacity to calculate probabilities and hence to assign the correct means to a given end." In modern times, subjective reason has begun to separate itself from its dialectical antithesis, namely, from the concept of an objective reason that inheres, as their core principle, in the structures of reality. As dogmatic metaphysics, this objective reason is indeed false. Yet subjective reason regresses into being an instrument for ends in relation to which it can no longer claim autonomy. For Horkheimer and Adorno, then, subjective instrumental rationality, in its absolute form, is as false as the dogmatic rationality it would replace; it expels the very last thought of a qualitative definition of the facts independent of preordained subjective goals. The need to dominate nature ultimately drives out the need to know nature objectively, even though the two needs had been inseparable from the outset. The dialectic of knowledge and projection, described by Nietzsche as the aporia of rational metaphysics and analyzed by Adorno in his critique of the philosophy of origins, has come to a standstill in the subjective reason of modernity.

However, the critique of rationality in negative dialectics does not itself depart from the framework of rationality. It demonstrates that the fusion of reason and domination leads ineluctably to the imposition of domination on all thinking. Thought can be sure of its object only through concepts, and the knowing subject can generate concepts only by disregarding the variety of qualities in an object, thereby making evident those qualities in the object that remain identical. This process of abstraction necessarily reduces the object to the signs of its identity and neglects what is nonidentical about it. In this manner, autonomous thinking can maintain the separateness of essence and appearance in its objects. Thus it can measure a reality structured by conceptual mediation through the rational viability embodied in it; only on this basis does it formulate a critique. Adorno's critique of rationality does not contest this liberating power of autonomous thinking. This power constitutes the basis on which thinking can reflect on its specific deficiency, which it cannot overcome by its own efforts. Thinking aims to recognize its objects by identifying what is essential in them. Yet, as Adorno shows, it is precisely this project that the process of identification itself ensures will fail. It falls short of its aims because it can always only define its objects as examples of something else, something general. But then it fails to say what the objects themselves are. The fact that conceptual thinking—and there is no other kind—cannot positively define what is nonidentical in objects of knowledge is the expression of an objective aporia. For Adorno, the nonidentical is not an "affirmative" concept that could be given definition, beyond the limits of rationality, through "other," nonrational modes of thinking. "The nonidentical cannot be directly accessed as something positive in itself. It is the conceptually negative result of the defined negation of the notion of identity."

Adorno describes this aporia, which logically consistent thinking cannot evade, as the paradoxical vanishing point of his own philosophical project. Alluding to Wittgenstein's philosophy of language, he writes, "If anything, philosophy should be defined as the effort to say that whereof one cannot speak: to help the nonidentical to be expressed, even as the act of expression assigns identity to it." Thinking always aims at the knowledge of something in its qualitative specificity, and it always misses its target. Therefore it must acknowledge its own insufficiency; it must admit to itself that, as the medium of the general, it can never quite reach the particular. Only then, in Adorno's view, can thinking free itself of its compulsive quality and acknowledge that, without the substratum of concepts that obstinately eludes systemic reduction, concepts remain empty. "To change the direction of conceptual thinking, to turn it toward the nonidentical—that is the hinge of negative dialectics. Confronted with the insight into the way the nonconceptual necessarily shapes all concepts, the identity compulsion afflicting all concepts lacking this counter-reflective moment would dissolve." Yet release from identity compulsion does not mean that the requirement of logical thinking has been suspended. Negative dialectics does not seek a "paradigm shift" that would discard rationality as a mere theatrical prop for the "grand narratives"—about which the storytellers of postmodernity, great and small, have meanwhile been talking ad nauseam. For Adorno, the nonidentical is not at all diffuse and unrelated to the numinous. Thus, the "coherence of the nonidentical" is accessible not through discarding logical categories but through overcoming the hypostasizing of classificatory conceptual structures that are often substituted for the materiality they represent. This overcoming is a moment of totality. "To grasp something in and for itself, not merely to install it in the conceptual framework, is in fact to access the individual moment in its immanent relationship to other moments." To Adorno, this recognition requires more, not less, rationality. "Philosophical reflection affirms the nonconceptual core of the concept."

In the spirit of *Minima Moralia*, Adorno defines the utopian core of a negative-dialectical philosophy: "the only philosophy that could still be affirmed in the face of despair" would be one that seeks "to view all things as they would be seen from the standpoint of redemption." The precarious, needy, distorted individual objects would no longer have to be subordinated to the ordering gesture of conceptual systematicity, but would instead recover their identity with the redemptive aid of concept and expression:

> Such a philosophy would have as its content the sheer variety of objects—a variety not mandated by any schema—that press in upon it, or that it seeks out; it would give itself wholly to the objects, not using them as a mirror in which it once again reads itself, confusing their image with their concrete being. This philosophy would be, quite simply, full and unmodified experience within the medium of conceptual reflection.

Such a philosophy aims to grasp "the nonidentical" as "the authentic identity of the object in opposition to its categorical identifications."

But how is that possible? Adorno aims to achieve it through the procedure of constellatory thinking. "Thinking does not have to be satisfied with its own structural laws; it is able to think against itself without betraying its own being." Moreover, "thinking against itself" will render achievable precisely that which thinking desires. When reason ceases to fixate on defining, through isolated concepts, what is presumed to be essential about objects conceptualized in isolation, and instead explores objects in their context, probing and describing them through variously combined concepts, then reason might gain gradual access to what the speculative framework of idealist philosophy had promised in vain. "The object opens itself to a sustained monadological pressure, which is the awareness of the constellation in which it is located. . . . Recognition of the object within its constellation is recognition of the material processes stored within it. And, also as a constellation, the theoretical process circles around the concept it seeks to open up." Thinking that could regulate its own movement according to the movement of objects, without having to give up its autonomy in such a quasi-mimetic rapprochement: that is Adorno's concrete conceptual utopia, accessible only via the path of immanent critique. Cognition thus becomes an open-ended process: "The ascertainable deficiency of all concepts mandates the citation of others: in this act those constellations arise which alone retain something of the hope contained in the act of naming. The language of philosophy draws close to this naming by negating its own abstraction."

Here again, defined negation. Concepts represent what is general about individual objects; names represent what is specific about them. Hence, speaking theologically and aesthetically, the counterideal to conceptual language is the language of naming. In the language of the Creator God and his name-giver Adam, there is for every living being, and for every thing, a single, immutable name, which expresses unmistakably the essence unique to it. This mythological conception of the magically identifying naming power of language gains a specific meaning when it is invoked as a corrective to that modern conception of language wherein words are no longer "bearers of substantive meaning" but are mere "signs without quality," unable to "bring the object into the realm of experience." Yet Adorno knows that a theory affirming the language of naming would merely fall behind the achievement of thinking's enlightened self-reflection.[1] His goal is thus to rescue the Aristotelian impulse to grasp what is individual by incorporating these impulses into his theory of constellatory conceptual thinking. For, he writes, "today as in Kant's time philosophy demands the critique of reason by means of reason, not by banishing or discarding it."

For Adorno, however, philosophy alone is not in a position to realize his critical utopia. In the shape of constellatory thinking it is already abandoning its inherited framework and opening itself to new forms of philosophical experience. Like Alexander Baumgarten, the founder of systematic philosophical aesthetics, Adorno views art as a genuinely "other" mode of cognition and seeks its support in the quest for an unedited experience of things as they are. It has therefore been assumed that Adorno, in his *Aesthetic Theory*, resignedly completed "the handing over to art of ultimate cognitive powers." Yet this is not at all the case. Another familiar reading of Adorno is equally mistaken about his core concern: namely, the view that he sought to blur the boundaries between philosophy and art, that his theme was "the aestheticizing of theory." This too is incorrect. In fact, Adorno's thesis is that "art's role in cognition" is possible because the two are inwardly linked while being fundamentally distinct. Works of art are characterized by the dialectical "configuration of mimesis and rationality." They contain knowledge which is not conceptually unified because it is bound to mimesis and to expressivity. Yet this cognitive potential is accessible only via conceptual reflection: "The truth content of artworks is the objective solving of the puzzle posed by each one individually. By insisting on a solution the puzzle points to the truth content. That truth is accessible only through philosophical reflection." Reflection, that is to say, thinking and its modality of concepts, always presupposes "something thought, something nonconceptual and nonidentical." Reflection must never forget that.

5

The Totally Socialized Society

ADORNO'S GOAL IS NOT the elimination of the concept of identity, but the rescue of the perspective of successful identity. This project implies a twofold sublimation of identity: a utopian negation both of existing nonidentity and inner contradiction and of the identity compulsion that is their reverse side. For a long time, Adorno argues, "society has impinged on every individual primarily as nonidentity, as compulsion." Hence the concept of the nonidentical possesses for him a dialectical double meaning. Its second meaning refers to that which eludes the compulsion to identity. Whether the nonidentical, in this latter sense, "actually exists" is by no means certain for Adorno. He understands it by analogy to the Marxist concept of use value. In modern commodified society, based on the production of goods, both things and people have social value, in the final analysis, only to the extent that they embody exchange value. On the quantitative scale of exchange value, use value appears artificial and historically irrelevant. Adorno summarizes: "The all-dominating principle of identity, namely, the abstract comparability of their social labor, drives human beings toward the extinction of their identity."

The Concept of Society

If philosophy is to demonstrate that it "needs what is not subsumed in social identity, namely, use value, in Marxist terminology," then it must change its procedures. That is, philosophy has an inherent tendency to transform itself into social theory. Adorno writes, "Only the social self-awareness of reflection gives it access to the objectivity which it lacks so long as it operates within the prevailing social forces without including them in its thought processes. Critique of society is critique of knowledge and vice versa." In critical theory, society is no mere functional concept but, above all, a structural one. Adorno's sociological writings have a philosophy of society at their core, for they are committed to "the ideal of grasping the essence of things." The concept of society is philosophical because it starts from two premises: first, it operates in accordance with laws, and second, these laws both are fundamental to the manifest variety of social realities and function on the surface of those realities. "A dialectical theory of society assumes structural laws that condition the facts, become evident in the facts, and are modified by those facts. Such a theory views these structural laws as tendencies that derive more or less strictly from the historical elements that have conditioned the overall system."

With this definition, Adorno gives a new critical shape to the old metaphysical distinction between essence and appearance. The "essential laws of society and its processes are more real than the factual surface in which they become manifest—but which always distorts them. Yet they jettison the essential attributes they bring with them. They can thus be named, in conceptual terms, as the very negativity which makes the world what it is." The essence of modern society, which simultaneously manifests itself and conceals itself, is something monstrous. This insight has both descriptive and normative significance. Essence is not ontologically substantive. It is not something that has metaphysical existence, but an abstraction that is tangibly present. Moreover, as the ongoing "essence" of society, this monstrous abstraction is identical with what is false: namely, that which prevents the realization of the "essence" of the human species.

Adorno's social theory aims to grasp the identity of society, its essence, while simultaneously subjecting it to critique as a compulsion to identity, as the negation of essence, in order to demonstrate that a compulsion-free identity, for both society and individuals, has yet to be realized.

The logic of the overall social process obeys not human goals but the abstract dynamics of economic expansion. Following Marx, Adorno argues that the structural law of modern society is grounded in the relationship of exchange between competing, legally organized partners, who are relevant qua individuals only with regard to their economic roles. Thus central economic maxims of Marxist theory are relevant to Adorno's critical social theory. The law of value, the "general law of capitalist accumulation," and "the general trend toward a drop in profit margins": these are defined as "Marxian models" for social theoretical "structural laws." In the present framework, Marx's labor theory of value cannot be discussed in detail. Its problems, apparent nowadays, must be left open for the moment. The important point is that although Adorno took up the Marxian theory of value, he did so in a way that ensured his ideas do not depend on it.

For Adorno, as for Marx, surplus value is created when wage labor is subsumed under capital. When the capacity for work is turned into a commodity, it has, for the owner of the means of production, a single utility value—it can produce more value than is needed in order to reproduce it as the producer's capacity for work. That is to say, its utility value is greater than its exchange value, which the worker receives in the form of wages. In this observation, for Adorno, lies the secret of exchange, which, in bourgeois society, is at once formally fair and materially unfair. Marx shows, in Adorno's words, "that in this society everything proceeds with fairness, that equivalent values really are exchanged—except in one decisive area, namely, where the commodity of capacity for work is involved: there the process is simultaneously fair and unfair." The core element of unpaid surplus labor is reflected in the produced goods as surplus value, which then, in the marketplace, can be realized as profit when the goods are sold. This exploitation of human value—here Adorno develops Marx's insight—is the "automatic subject," hence the driver of social dynamics: a dynamic, he adds, that is ultimately barely distinguishable from stasis, since social production is defined not primarily by the needs of people, but by the requirement of exploitation. That is how capitalist accumulation operates, but this structural fact does not generate the collapse of the social and economic system, which Marx and his orthodox successors had viewed as the necessary consequence of the general trend toward a drop in the average profit margins of capitalist enterprises.

When Adorno speaks of the negativity of the social essence, he is doing so within a Marxian framework. This negativity resides in the irreconcilable conflict of the groups constituting society and operates within individual psychologies. Hence Adorno speaks affirmingly of "a negative ontology of society grounded in antagonistic processes," which he sees as implicit in Marx. With this language he alludes to Marx's summation of history as a story of class struggles.[1] Adorno stresses that Marx's class theory cannot simply be applied to the present, for it is centered on the concept of class consciousness. To be sure, he says, "one cannot today speak of a proletarian class consciousness within the normative capitalist countries." But that does not mean giving up on the concept of class as an instrument of economic diagnosis. The absence of class consciousness "does not, despite common opinion to the contrary, itself refute the existence of classes: class was defined by the relation to the means of production, not by the consciousness of its members." For Adorno, the crucial element is a dialectical concept of the conflicting basic versions of society, which he grasps in a metaeconomic way. It is essential to conceptualize social "structure, which has been antagonistic since the inception of society as such, and which always remained so, as foreign policy conflicts and the permanent possibility of catastrophic war glaringly demonstrate." Critical theory cannot attain certainty about the transition to a society liberated from the pressures of the exploitation of value; this lack of certainty reflects its distance from Marx's economically based theory of revolution, which Adorno criticizes for its unintentional relapse into an idealist philosophy of history. Adorno writes, "Marx's expectation that the priority of productive forces was historically certain and would necessarily rupture the relations of production—this expectation was all too optimistic. To this extent Marx, the sworn enemy of German idealism, remained faithful to its positive construction of history."

In the postwar world, German academic sociology mostly held in contempt the subtleties of dialectical social philosophy. For example, René König declared that in both Marxism and the critical theory of Horkheimer and Adorno, "eschatological prophecies are fused with visions of the last days." He found fault with "the metaphysical exaggeration" resulting from "the speculative character of the concept of society underlying this whole way of thinking," because this concept was oriented toward the goal of free association among all working people. In König's view, "it suffices to abandon this concept in order for all the consequences derived from it to become obsolete." Evidently he viewed the abandonment of the dialectical conception of society as scientific progress. The results of this process became clear in the 1960s, when, in the "dispute over positivism in German sociology," similar arguments were leveled against Adorno and Habermas by the value-neutral, scientistic school of Karl Popper. However, the critical theorists were able to demonstrate that positivist theories of social systems engage in functionalist categorical limiting that leads to a loss of understanding of both experience and reality in the social sciences.

Positivist perspectives misread the specific approach whereby the metaphysical element is transformed both in Marx and in critical theory. At a time when the terms "speculation" and "metaphysics" had not yet been reduced to insults for attacking mere guesses and weird supernatural ideas, it was assumed that speculation was simply synonymous with an intellectual theoretical viewpoint, and that metaphysics was the conceptual process of defining the principles of being in their totality. We have already shown, in the account of Adorno's immanent critique of idealism, that he is not pursuing speculative metaphysics in the old style. His point was that the spiritual contemplation of everything that is was always derived from first principles of an assumed divine or ideal transcendence. But, on the other hand, Adorno is clear that we cannot manage intellectually without the distinction between being and appearance—unless we want to abandon ourselves without concepts to the sheer variety of social phenomena and thereby become incapable of critique. Contrary to Wittgenstein's formula that claims to reduce the world of the knowing subject to everything that is factual, Adorno argues, "Metaphysics is the structure of consciousness wherein it attempts to know what is more than factual—or what is not merely factual yet must be engaged by consciousness, because what we call the facts compel us to do so." As long as the social essence conceals itself behind society's surface manifestations, thus eluding possible change in accordance with humane goals, metaphysics's claim to know truth remains unsatisfied:

> Essence is what is concealed by the social laws that oppose it; to argue that there is no essence is to take the side of appearance as such, namely, totalizing ideology, which is absorbing ever more dimensions of existence. Whoever views all appearances as equal, because he knows of no essence that would authorize distinctions, is making—through an uncompromising love of "truth"—common cause with untruth.

How little Adorno is concerned with affirmative metaphysics, and the extent to which he made himself independent of the Marxist doctrine of labor value, becomes clear from another intellectual move: he considers the possibility that current critical theory, in contradistinction to Marx, can perhaps no longer begin with a critique of immanent facts, because, although laws of social structure still prevail, they may no longer manifest themselves consistently as they did in the era of the flourishing bourgeois society. In 1969 he wrote,

> The key element of Marxist theory, the theory of surplus value, was supposed to explain class relations and the growth of class antagonism in objective economic terms. If, however, the involvement of living labor, from which alone, in Marx's perspective, surplus value flows, becomes reduced to a marginal role by the sheer range of technical progress, in effect by industrialization, then the core element of surplus value is affected. The current absence of an objective theory of value is conditioned not only by the establishing of an economics that is almost the only one to be accepted academically. The lack reminds

us of the prohibitive difficulty of objectively theorizing class formation without the theory of surplus value.... It is possible that contemporary society eludes any theory coherent in itself. Marx had it easier, insofar as the fully developed liberal system was ready for scientific analysis. He needed only to ask whether capitalism, within its own dynamic categories, corresponds to this model, in order to generate a comparably consistent counter-theory in explicit negation of the theoretical system confronting him. But since then the market economy has become so full of holes that it mocks any such theoretical confirmation. The irrationality of today's social structure prevents its rational translation into theory.

Adorno has no unambiguous answers to the questions that he raises in this passage. But it is precisely his lack of definite or easy answers that speaks for his theory, which does not seal itself off from the social and economic upheavals that critical theory confronts today.

In *Negative Dialectics*, Adorno goes even further. First he uses the concept of freedom to situate the program, the claim made by modern bourgeois society, in the context of its contrasting reality. Then he reflects on the dialectic hidden in the very concept of social order:

> The society according to whose precepts human relations are to be grounded in freedom—although until now freedom has not been actualized in its relationships—this society is as rigid as it is defective. In a relationship of universal barter, all those qualitative elements whose essence might constitute structure get flattened out. The more excessive the power of institutional structures, the more chaotic the life that they confine and deform according to their image. The production and reproduction of life, together with everything contained in the concept of superstructure, do not render intelligible the one rationality that, when realized, would define an order worthy of humanity, namely, order without force. The old, organic social orders are either obsolete or outliving their legitimacy for the benefit of evil. Nowhere does society function in any way as anarchically as can appear in the irrational, chance elements of an individual's existence. But society's reified conformity to a rigid structure is the counterpart of a concept of existence in which living would be liberated from anxiety.

For Adorno, chaos is legible as a figure encoded in order. He gives a radical description of the breaking apart of rational human potential and the irrational reality of modern society, the contradictory interplay between anomic decay and institutionally intensified rigidity. In this process, poststructuralist insights are anticipated and also relativized dialectically. The logic of social decay is revealed only by deconstruction, but this logic is one of institutionally objectified stasis; deconstruction is conceived not as a mere philosophical technique but effectively as the negative movement of society and its economic basis.

From today's perspective one must express reservations about an assumption repeatedly formulated by Horkheimer and Adorno: that the world is ever more "administered," indeed, that it might one day be totally administered. At least on the global scale, one can assert that society, in many areas, is "functioning as anarchically as can appear in the irrational, chance elements of an individual's existence." Today's crises, civil wars, and migrations suggest that the integrative power of the world economic order, with its impulse toward a global society, is declining dramatically. To that extent, one cannot simply apply the thesis of an administered world as a critical theory appropriate to today's society. But it can be viewed as a theoretical template, against which the present tendency toward the failure of integrative efforts stands out as a historical moment in a process that must be reconstructed dialectically, namely, the contradictory interplay between globalization and the internal decay of societies ruled by the market economy.

Liquidation of the Individual

In modern social philosophy, the individual's potential for either development or decline is located between the poles of freedom and order; this is so even in the counter-versions, the social utopias that Ernst Bloch systematized in accordance with these core concepts. For Adorno, the antithesis of successful mediation between general and individual interest is the totally socialized society. To the end, his analytical and critical work was devoted to dissecting this phenomenon. His theory of the individual is developed in this context. It also engages the question of how the individual's free development and satisfaction of needs could be reconciled with the rational and nonrepressive order of a putative social whole. But that is not its main theme, for Adorno's theory of the individual is a negative theory, which begins by conceptualizing the failure of these attempts at mediation, whether they are shaped by affirmative description or by utopian normativity: "If hope remains in the administered world, it lies not in the mediation efforts but at the extremes."

In critical theory, the individual is understood not as a timeless anthropological category but as historically conditioned.

> What "individual" specifically means . . . is not defined by the biological entity. The individual is crystallized by, in a sense, defining itself and by elevating its own singularity, its self-containedness, into its true reason for being. In earlier times both the language of philosophy and that of the everyday labeled this as "self-consciousness." Only he who differentiates himself from the interests and strivings of others, who becomes his own essence and establishes his self-assertion and development as the norm, is an individual.[2]

However, Adorno does not view the category of individual as the polar opposite of the social. Rather, critical theory inquires into the "dynamics of the individual's self-construction," which reveals itself to be "socially mediated." It is only in modernity that the individual constructs itself as a social entity, as a direct result of that decay of the universal order of the Middle Ages, which instigates the process whereby the free, self-defining individual person becomes the generator of economic and cultural change. Adorno summarizes:

> When the free-market economy displaced the feudal system and needed both entrepreneur and free wage laborer, these human types constructed themselves not only occupationally but also anthropologically; concepts emerged such as responsibility for oneself, predictive power, the self-sufficient individual, fulfillment of obligations—but also rigid requirements of conscience and internalized subservience to authorities. The individual, as we still use the term today, dates in its specifics hardly any further back than Montaigne or Hamlet, certainly not earlier than the beginnings of the Italian Renaissance.

Without falling back into a mirror theory, Horkheimer and Adorno study the career of the individual as a social process defining modernity against the background of the transition of the liberal moment into a capitalist society structured first on authoritarian lines, then with democratic forms—administered, however, through bureaucratic and technological methods. From the beginning, as they make clear in the sociological excursuses that were published collectively in the 1950s by the reborn Institute for Social Research, "the bourgeois individual is tyrannized by oppositions, like that between personal and public political existences, and between private and professional spheres of life. With economic political development, these oppositions intensified." The concept of bourgeois individuality is highly ideological: that is, it is simultaneously true and false. It embodies society's historically developing structural laws and is loaded down with legitimating assumptions and norms to which individuals, as actually existing humans, cannot possibly do justice.

> The enthronement of the principle of competition, when guilds dissolved and the industrial revolution began, installed in bourgeois society a dynamic that compels the individual economic agent to pursue ruthlessly his drive toward acquisition, unconcerned about the general good. The Protestant ethic and the bourgeois capitalist concept of duty enlisted the drive of the individual conscience to this end. The antifeudal ideal of individual autonomy, originally focused on political self-determination, was transformed by the economic process into the ideology required by that process for maintaining order and maximizing achievement. Thus, to the completely self-absorbed individual, reality becomes appearance and appearance reality. By defining his isolated existence—one which is dependent on society, indeed only conditionally tolerated by it—as absolute, the individual makes himself into a pure verbal construct, into the "unique" entity defined by [Max] Stirner.

Adorno's critical analysis of the individual as ideological construct shows, first, that the individual is not some ultimate natural essence and, second, that it is a socially produced form of bourgeois subjectivity that is not only historically defined but also, for that very reason, transitional and ephemeral. As Adorno puts it, "Today competition and the free-market economy are losing ever more weight in the face of concentrated corporate structures and the collective relationships imposed by them. The concept of the individual . . . is reaching its historical limit."

In Adorno's work there are two different versions of what will happen when this limit is reached. In the 1940s he supports Horkheimer's "theory of rackets," which argues that contemporary society is characterized by the irrevocable elimination of the individual. According to the racket theory, the social structure of the advanced industrial nations is politically totalitarian and shaped economically by either monopolies or state capitalism. The theory characterizes social interest groups as rival "racketeers." They protect their members but demand unconditional subservience. In struggles for shares of the wealth, which are more or less openly conducted, they strive for the maintenance and increase of their living standards, as well as for social dominance, and they divide social influence antagonistically among themselves. In this view, the individual can maintain his social ranking only by belonging to the appropriate racket, that is, by inherently tending toward renouncing his own individuality. "Self-preservation means loss of self": that is Adorno's formula for this process in *Minima Moralia*. No longer farsightedness, autonomy, and spontaneity: rather, adaptability and conformity become the qualities of character essential to survival, regardless of which "racket" one belongs to, whether it is the CEO's network, the political power clique, or the trade union. The individual is liquidated.

Racket theory evocatively captured specific qualities of postliberal society in the advanced countries of the first half of the twentieth century—much as Brecht's play *The Resistible Rise of Arturo Ui* captured elements of National Socialism for literature. The problem with racket theory is, first, its insufficient ability to differentiate particular groups appropriately and, second, its economic assumptions. It stands or falls with the accuracy of the premise that the twentieth century is the age of monopoly capitalism, regardless of whether it is structured in a seemingly democratic or outright fascistic way or is replaced by state socialism. Yet the liquidation of the sphere of circulation, the elimination of competition, the replacement of the anarchic production of goods by a command economy—in reality none of these outcomes occurred. And even the state-socialist planned economy of the Eastern bloc remained oriented toward the competition of the world market, which ultimately, as we know, combined with its own structural failings to finish it off.

At the Institute for Social Research, after the war, scholars no longer worked with the theory of rackets and state capitalism. Adorno also soon renounced this model, which clearly did not describe actual development adequately. In order to align the content of experience theoretically with the idea that, in our time, the individual is no longer society's indispensable element, Adorno investigated a phenomenon that became dominant after the war and remains so to this day: the renewed blossoming of "individualism," which critical theory shows to be a socially essential illusion.

Throughout his intellectual life, Adorno understands his theory of the individual to be at once critique and rescue: critique of the hypostasized principle of individuation and rescue of the authentic human content saved up within that principle. Paradoxically, this content can be made fruitful only in the historical moment when the principle of individuation seems about to lose its value entirely. In *Minima Moralia*, the point is to grasp hold of the individual's potential for resistance at the very moment when this category is about to lose its substance. In Adorno's later writings, on the other hand, he demonstrates the ideological element in invoking the individual's authority at a time when individuality is again being hypostasized.

In *Minima Moralia*, he writes,

> The questions concerning individuality must be asked again in the age of its liquidation. Whereas the individual, like all individualist production processes, has fallen behind the state of technological development and has become a historical relic, in its very role as the victor's victim it is again the necessary bearer of truth. For only the individual retains, in however distorted a form, the trace of that which alone justifies technological processes, and which indeed these processes structurally repress. Insofar as unrestricted progress reveals itself to be not identical with the progress of humanity, true progress can be given secret shelter by its opposite.

The individual is no longer contemporary, overtaken by the progress which it itself generated. The social principle of individuation impelled itself toward "the victory of fatalism," that is, toward its own extinction. The anachronistic quality of the principle of individuation is, for critical theory, an ambivalent result: a society freed from the blind profit motive and oriented toward reason and justice would recognize as false the fetishizing of the bourgeois category of individuality, and would find other forms of humane socialization. Accordingly, a substantive advance would be one that actually transcended the principle of individuation. But the "advance" that is occurring is in fact no advance at all, because it does no justice to the conceptual challenge: it merely negates abstractly the values it pushes aside. The tendency toward the sheer extinction of the principle of individuation falls back behind what has been achieved historically and the promise it contained.

When Adorno turns, thematically and methodologically, to the individual and its specific experiential forms, he does so not from nostalgic mourning of the loss of bourgeois subjectivity but because only from such a perspective can one retain the intellectual power of resistance that, philosophically, seizes the perspective of nonidentity and, as a theory of society, will not part with the telos of free self-determination. Adorno writes,

> The individual has gained as much in fullness, differentiation, and strength as it has lost through being weakened and hollowed out by the standardized society. In its era of decay, the individual's experience of itself and what is happening to it contributes once more to an understanding that had simply been hidden for as long as the individual viewed itself, with undiminished affirmation, as the ruling social category. Confronted by totalitarian uniformity, which the process of eliminating difference clearly announces as its goal, the individual sphere may even have temporarily drawn into itself something of society's power to liberate. It is in that sphere that critical theory lingers—and not just with a bad conscience.

Such experiences put critical theory into a position where it can understand the pseudoindividuality of the present for what it is; as

Adorno writes, "The fewer individuals, the more individualism." In a critical perspective, individualism describes a person who is dominated by society's structural rules: that is, a person who lies within the framework of prescribed consumption and the organized filling out of free time by the culture industry, by sport, and by enthusiasm for technology. For Adorno, integration, traditionally evoked by sociology as existing in a tension-ridden relationship with drives to differentiation within societies, has become an autonomous force in the administered world. Total integration, for him, means the complete standardization of human beings, including their subjectivity:

> Humans' adaptation to social relations and processes, which constitutes history and without which their continued existence would have been difficult, is so deeply embedded in them that the possibility of breaking out of it, even just in their minds, without unbearable subjective conflicts, is dwindling. Embodying the triumph of integration, they identify, even in their most intimate behavior patterns, with the role the world assigns them. . . . The process lives off the fact that human beings also owe their lives to what is being done to them. The social cement that ideologies used to provide has, on the one hand, shifted into the overwhelming presence of social relations as such, and, on the other, has infiltrated human beings' actual psychological constitution.

In psychoanalysis, the rational understanding of one's own psychic structure was supposed to open the way to an autonomous life free of neurotic distortions. Freud wanted to make individual psychology transparent as the complex interplay of instructions issued by the psychic apparatus. The contradictory unity that must be generated in the ego as a mediation between the libidinal drives of the id and the normative claims of the superego is precarious. The balance in the ego between the demands of the libido and the self-control mandated by the social compulsions internalized as conscience is constantly under threat of collapse. In Hans-Martin Lohmann's formulation, psychoanalysis becomes the "party representative of the repressed, culturally outlawed impulses," because it demystifies them, decodes their mechanisms and structural economy, and shows individuals how they, through self-understanding, can spare themselves suffering. Psychoanalysis is simultaneously "science of the unconscious" and "method of treatment." From the doctrine of the painful return of the repressed in the individual psyche it derives information about the return of the repressed on the scale of human culture as a whole, and reconstructs our violent, conflict-laden history on the basis of material provided by myths. Freud's rationalist credo reads: Where the id was, there the ego shall be. That goal is not perpetuation, but self-conscious breaking and sublimation of the compulsion that culture has imposed on human beings to this day, without lasting success. "The human spirit, itself derived from nature, does not have to sit in judgment on the 'dark impulses'; rather, it is to be the authority that opens itself to the 'darkness' and is thereby in a position to control its disturbing presence. For only when the human being's impulse-driven nature is neither denied nor broken by the imperialism of reason does the possibility exist of escaping the false alternative of bondage to nature and cultural hypocrisy." Here Adorno emphatically links his thinking to Freud's achievement, which he sees as the naming of the excessive suffering that a repressive society imposes on individuals.

This naming results in an irrefutable portrayal of society's antagonistic essence, as it is mirrored in the suffering of its members. When psychoanalysis shows that the ego is not master in its own house, it presents the fragility of individuation as if from an inside perspective. Freud uncovers the inner nonidentity of the individual and the suffering that occurs precisely because no rational self-identity exists. But, in Adorno's view, the very attempt to produce this rational self causes psychoanalysis to fall behind its own insights. The uncompromising quality of psychoanalysis is to be defended against all attempts to take the sting out of it in order to modulate it back into a usable therapeutic formula. Such a formula would no longer have as its radical starting point human psychological drives and the aporias of a socializing process that cannot satisfy these drives; it would, instead, make lazy compromises in order to restore suffering human beings' ability to function, by eliminating their painful awareness of suffering, not the suffering itself. However, in Adorno's eyes, both the "revised" version of psychoanalysis and authentic psychoanalysis itself have features of a mere repair operation. The inherent claim of the latter to restore individuals' capacity for both work and pleasure, is, for Adorno, bourgeois ideology by definition, at least so long as it does not confront the necessity of radically transforming social relations that structurally prevent us from taking pleasure in work. As Adorno wrote, "Nothing is true about psychoanalysis but its exaggerations." As to the therapeutic function of psychoanalysis, Adorno demands nothing less than "a cathartic method that would be required, not to define itself by successful adaptation and economic satisfaction, but to bring human beings to an awareness of true unhappiness, of the public condition and of their own which is inseparable from it; the method would need to abolish the illusions of satisfaction through which the disgusting social order retains its psychic power in humans' minds, as if it did not already sufficiently control them externally." In an individual context, that certainly sounds bleak. Adorno's claim, however, must be seen in the context of the efforts of the Institute for Social Research to undermine the conformist element of the psychoanalytic approach by transforming the psychoanalysis of the individual into an analytic social psychology. The normative basis of Adorno's (sometimes unfair[3]) criticisms of Freud is the proposed integration of Freudian and Marxist theory.

To be sure, in *Dialectic of Enlightenment* the limits of this undertaking are made clear. Horkheimer and Adorno, as already stated, attempt in that work to define the limited scope of social-psychological enlightenment using its own methods. For them, the fact that the ultimate manifestation of archaic anti-Semitism occurred in a modernity shaped by science and technology signifies a new dimension of social repression. Human beings' self-identification with the social principle that dominates them becomes total and demands a projective shift to the external world; in the pogrom, where power rules, the individual's regressive rebellion against the prescribed renunciation of drives has been incorporated into the very laws governing social behavior.

The historical experience embodied in the name *Auschwitz* lends additional weight to Adorno's theory of the liquidation of the individual. In the concentration camps it was not the historical-philosophical construction of the individual that was liquidated, but actual individuals. They were literally liquidated; but first they were de-individualized, reduced to mere numbered examples of species, and all that occurred within a space of integrated structure and quantification that metamorphosed into something completely new. In *Negative Dialectics*, Adorno illuminated this space from the opposite perspective: it is not the social expropriation of the individual's destiny but the expropriation even of his dying, destroying even the appearance of life's meaning as a coherent whole, that seals the loss of humane, autonomous subjectivity:

> Through the administrative murder of millions, death became something that had never hitherto threatened in such a form. There was no longer the possibility that it could enter the life experienced by an individual as somehow in harmony with life's course. The individual is stripped of the ultimate, most minimal property that had been his own. The fact that, in the camps, specimens died rather than individuals, influences the fates of all those who escaped the actual extermination. Mass murder is the process of absolute integration, in preparation wherever human beings are de-individualized, a process refined, as was said in the military, until they, their very existence defined as a deviation from their total nothingness, are literally exterminated.

Adorno's ideological-critical analysis of the birth of the principle of individuation can today be compared with Foucault's analytical reconstruction of the discourse compelling the disciplining of the human being's inner nature in the process of transition to modernity. The notion of the end of the individual, in which Adorno's theory of individuation culminates, conceptualizes a similarly specific social experience. But it also shares the danger that it gives a falsely definitive coloration to facts that have a specific historical context—if it portrays the end of the individual as the result of an irreversible process. The problem with such a perspective is that it can eliminate ruptures and historical discontinuities, and thereby eliminate moments and locations of resistance to the norm. This is not Adorno's intention; he does not endorse the culturally conservative lament about the "loss of individuality,"[4] but seeks to deploy the strength of the individual that becomes tangible at the very moment when it is threatened with disappearance. But if that disappearance is no longer defined as a theoretical tendency, but rather is crystallized as a definitive condition, then the dialectic of the principle of individuation would necessarily also be brought to a standstill.[5] However, Adorno did not draw that conclusion; even in his last writings he endeavored to render transparent the dialectic of the principle of individuation, persisting in its virulence, so that the opposing idea of social autonomy could be brought into view.

Critical Theory on Morality

The project of social autonomy is a kind of projection of the normative idea of individual autonomy, simultaneously concrete and utopian, that had developed as a core concept of the philosophy of the Enlightenment. In exile during the Second World War, Adorno meditated on the "possibility of living." After describing the aesthetic aporia of modernity, he argued that there is no longer such a thing as undamaged "private life." According to Adorno, the avant-garde utopia of a stylistically authentic, functional shaping of life grounded in the spirit of modernity had been shattered. Years earlier, Benjamin had praised the architecture and design of classical modernism for possessing "decency" without aura, and asserted its embodiment of "a new, positive concept of barbarism." In contrast to Benjamin's praise was Bloch's polemic of a few years earlier still: obstetric forceps should perhaps be smooth and without ornament, but sugar tongs should not. As Bloch saw it, just because one particular tool should, because of functional necessity, be free of decoration, it by no means follows that another tool, serving quite different purposes, should be ascetically purified of all semiotic and aesthetic connotations. Bloch portrayed the transparent architecture of modernism, which allowed no one to hide, as a single, huge glass training camp for the fascist dictatorship of surveillance. In contrast to Bloch, Adorno argued that all attempts from *within* bourgeois capitalist society to reform the shape and appearance of daily life were condemned to failure. An aesthetically authentic life was possible only within a liberated society. Because social revolution had been neglected in the West, one could really "no longer live." The destruction of European cities by bombing attacks and the National Socialist labor and concentration camps both confirm a single tendency, one being implemented universally, namely, the tendency toward scientific-technical maximization of efficiency in the capitalist production of goods.

Although Adorno did not say so explicitly, he clearly viewed modernist ideals such as Le Corbusier's concept of the house as a "machine for living" as manifestations of a technocratic-instrumental rationality. Nor did Adorno endorse the comfortable nonculture of self-indulgent suburbia. And Heidegger's anti-urban model of the hut in the Black Forest was equally out of the question. In Adorno's opinion, it had become clear that the functionalist revolt against ornament had turned into an "autonomous" aesthetic dogma. Functionalism doesn't function, he argued in his famous speech "Functionalism Today," which he delivered to the German Workers' League in Berlin in 1965. The appropriate response to the failure of functionalism is not to make existential decisions about life forms, but to recognize a paradox. On the one hand, it is sheer pretentiousness to shape one's life according to aesthetically autonomous criteria while clinging to the ideal of private property. On the other hand, indifference to shaping life aesthetically indicates only an inability to grasp things with libidinal spontaneity. Moreover, this indifference is complementary to the inability to treat human beings with love, a dual reinforcing Adorno's insights into the authoritarian character. Adorno felt that, in light of this paradox, the best we could do was to behave in a "nonbinding, suspended" way: "to continue private life for as long as the social order and one's own needs permit no alternative, but not to burden it as if it were still socially essential and individually appropriate." In the context of this reflection on the antinomies of living, Adorno formulated one of his best-known maxims, one that very soon afterwards was interpreted as the axiom of his negative moral philosophy: "There is no true life within the false." Adorno himself later acknowledged as legitimate the transference of his a priori conclusion from aesthetics and social theory to the realm of ethics. At the start of his Frankfurt lecture "Problems of Moral Philosophy," delivered in the 1950s, he noted that the students might well wonder how the author of this sentence could plan to discuss ethical questions with them for a whole semester. At the end of the lecture, having articulated the principles of ancient Greek ethics and intensively engaged Kantian moral philosophy, Adorno returned to his starting point and declared that, although he indeed had no moral-philosophical counsel to offer, he was completely prepared to present his own intellectual model. How could one, as an individual, live even halfway conscientiously when in the overall social context there was no such thing as a normatively just life—and hence no justice? His answer: the model of a "stand-in life."

The model of a stand-in life is a cautious revaluation of private life. Adorno proposed that "something like the models of just living be built from the closest relationships of human beings." By this he did not mean generating morally pure worlds in the niches of society (which he terms "late capitalist").[6] Rather, he imagined intersubjective relationships, in which the participants experience each other as partially free and self-defining; as capable of partial resistance against immorality, pseudomorality, or enforced morality; and as capable of partial solidarity against the abstract principle of self-preservation in the barter society. As much as possible, he argued, we should act toward one another "as one might imagine life would necessarily be conducted among liberated, peaceful human beings who feel themselves in solidarity." Adorno was aware of the limitations of this model. He thus defined it as the "powerless effort" of a "fragile, questionable, stand-in existence." Moreover, he had defined this project in similar terms in the 1940s, when he was contemplating the "last possibilities" of "generating humane cells within the inhumane social whole."

In the aphorism from *Minima Moralia* in which these words appear, the issue is the institution of marriage in the decaying bourgeois society. In light of the plentiful biographical information about Adorno that emerged in 2003, many a reader may have wondered whether the dictum that no true life is possible within a false framework was secretly conceived as a justification for immoral behavior. Adorno the husband rushing from one extramarital affair to the next, while his wife cries her eyes out at home: that is a "humane" model of a "representative existence"? In fact, the German press coverage during Adorno's centenary year (some of it reported with tangible satisfaction) did not accurately reflect reality. From the outset, the Adornos had a thoroughly nonbourgeois understanding about their marriage, assuring both of them complete erotic freedom. Evidently they both envisaged a free companionship, based on solidarity, that left space for other desires, resisted making one partner into a private possession of the other, and simultaneously shaped a protective zone against the intrusive pressures of a society both felt to be repressive. For a while, that worked for both of them. But with time an imbalance developed that can seem unjust. Arguably this is tied to certain customs of our culture, whereby older professors do not necessarily lose their attraction for younger members of the fair sex, while older women face greater difficulties in this area. Perhaps also it was a question of needs that diverged in individual ways over the years—or of something quite different, we cannot tell. Such biographical questions are irrelevant in this context.

In his later Frankfurt lecture on moral philosophy, given in the 1960s, Adorno completed, via an Aristotelian turn, the transition from ethics to political philosophy. At the end of the lecture he made the following remarks about the problematic concept of "living justly": "In short . . . whatever we may still call morality these days is indissolubly linked to the question of the structure of society. One could say: the question of the just life is the question of a just politics—if a just politics were today in the realm of what could actually be realized." Adorno was convinced that all moral-philosophical reflections in the Western tradition begin with the false assumption that individual action is free and autonomous and hence normatively either right or wrong. All moral-philosophical reflections, therefore, remain necessarily within the conceptual circle of an ideological illusion. In Adorno's words, they are "governed by the blanket clause of a private ethics." Consequently, the way forward consists either of a *political ethics* as the basis of a normatively just, collective praxis, or, so long as this route is blocked, of the ethics of noncooperation. In the "administered world" we are compelled to "play along," to conform. We cannot resist this compulsion, but even though we have to "play along," we at least should do so only with mental reservations.

I term this mode of thinking the "normative dualism" of Adorno's negative moral philosophy. The actual situation, although it defines what is possible for us as actors, must not be given the last word. It must not constitute the totality. Or, in a more current formulation: our expectations of normatively just behavior are the counterfactual standard that governs praxis. Adorno did not think of this standard as normativity. But his theoretical model of "defined negation" does not permit a monistic perspective on this field. It continues Kant's biworldly ethical doctrine, but points it in a negative direction. Within this framework, it is possible for Adorno to define the duality of moral philosophy. As he sees it, moral norms assert a general claim to validity that suppresses the specific impulses and emotions of active subjects. But a rational general perspective, wherein the specific impulses, emotions, and interests of all human subjects attain validity, is for him conceivable only on the basis of socially acknowledged moral insights.

Domination of the individual by social power and a rational general view: those are the two sides of Adorno's moral dualism. In Kant and Nietzsche, these two perspectives are polar opposites. For Kant moral action is based on freedom, while for Nietzsche morality is nothing but "perpetual constraint." Adorno fused these perspectives, but did not think of fusion as a Kierkegaardian or postmodern paradox that affirms the ongoing coexistence of opposites. In Adorno's view, freedom and compulsion are antithetical defining pressures within subjectivity itself. We should acknowledge the conflicting subjective forces in their contradictory being, but with the goal of overcoming the contradiction. It is unclear whether Adorno thinks this goal a regulative-epistemological base, as Kant believes, or defines a practical utopia, as Marx attempts to do.

Kant, in the context of his reflections on education, put the question thus: "How do I cultivate freedom when acting under pressure?" But he was convinced that this question, central to every educational process, could be answered through a calculation of means and ends. A certain degree of compulsion was needed in the education of the not-yet-rational child in order to enable rational behavior when the child reached maturity. What Kant views as a temporally limited phase in childhood development, Adorno defines as an ongoing process of mental causation: a process of negating the negation wherein freedom and compulsion are constantly being actualized through their impact on each other. Without at least partial lived freedom, we would have no concept of moral prescriptions, and certainly would be unable to observe them. But moral presumptions present themselves necessarily as imperatives, claiming not partial but unconditional universal validity. Their always particular origin has always already disappeared behind their universalizing validity claim. To the extent that moral prescriptions have an impact, it rests on their authority, which is guaranteed only by convention.

Adorno did not proceed, in the realm of moral philosophy, the way Carl Schmitt did in the philosophy of law: he did not say "force makes morality" in an analogy to Schmitt's maxim that "power prescribes law." Therein lies the difference between him and Michel Foucault. Adorno did not deny the rational love which moral principles always have. But he insisted that this rational core attains validity only by means of its antithesis, irrational force. As a result, moral reflection simultaneously grounds and restricts the individual's freedom of action. The realm of the mimetic impulse must be repressed. But because it is only as persons capable of action that we can ultimately articulate our interests, impulses, and mimetic reactions, morality is the forerunner of freedom precisely because of its role as instrument of repression.

For Adorno, this contradiction is inherent in living. European Christian morality educates people to feel a sense of responsibility and presumes a freedom of action that they absolutely do not have. At the same time, it is "representative of a coming freedom," for it offers normative standards of critique vis-à-vis the empirical behavior of people as they actually are. As a philosopher, then, one must be "both for and against morality." Critique of morality should point neither toward an affirmative countermorality nor toward the abstract negation of all morality, two opposing perspectives that had intersected in the work of Nietzsche. For Adorno, critique of morality is legitimate only when it is a "defined negation" of morality. Thus the critic "confronts morality with its own definition, so that the question is posed: is morality moral, does it do justice to its own principles?"

Normative dualism allows Adorno's negative moral philosophy to make use of zones of differentiation that, as far as I can see, are not available to more recent monistic ethical conceptions. To clarify this point, I offer now a few remarks on what Adorno means by his notion of normative dualism. The dualism between "private morality" in a "typical life" and a blocked-off "political ethic" is based on the dualism of Kant's moral philosophy between intelligible freedom and empirical unfreedom. Pragmatically, Adorno argues, we are not normally in a position to act in a morally just way. But that by no means implies that we should let go of the counterfactual standard that, if we allow ourselves to be corrupted, speaks loud and clear to our conscience. In other words: as an affirmative ethics of rigorous imperatives, the moral philosophy of Western Christian rationality is doomed to failure. But as a definition of difference from what is actually the case, and as a critical standard for what could be, it is the best we have in the field of practical philosophy.

This critical dualism within practical philosophy corresponds to the heuristic distinction between appearance and essence in Western metaphysics. Fully twenty years after his reflections on living and the just behavioral life, Adorno formulated, in *Negative Dialectics*, a statement of solidarity with the fallen metaphysics that he had earlier substantiated thoroughly in a Frankfurt lecture. Simplified, the essence of the argument runs as follows: whoever can no longer distinguish between essence and appearance is no longer able to speak, for example, of "late capitalism," but only of industrialized society; not of exploitation through capitalist surplus value, but only of social partnership and the interests of political positions. Although Adorno did not put it this way, it would be wholly in his spirit to say that whoever, like the contemporary philosopher Richard Rorty, prefers no longer to distinguish between appearance and essence has, strictly speaking, no conceptual tool with which to oppose human beings who treat others inhumanely. If we are to oppose the persecution of witches, to oppose racism and the politics of apartheid, the fundamental essence of the human being as a creature endowed with reason (or, in Ernst Cassirer's words, as *animal symbolicum*) becomes indispensable, with everything that follows from it for our concept of human dignity. According to Adorno, the term "metaphysics" "means on the one hand the engagement with metaphysical themes, even when their metaphysical content is contested; on the other hand it denotes the affirmative doctrine of a higher world in the Platonic tradition." Only affirmative metaphysics is affected by Nietzsche's verdict against the "backward" assumption of "other" worlds said to be the only fully real ones. (This polemical wordplay makes use of the similar sounds of the German words *wäldlerisch* and *weltlerisch* and suggests that philosophical metaphysicians have a reactionary outlook comparable to that of hillbillies or lumberjacks). Nietzsche's verdict, however, is rebounding off the reflective postmetaphysical thinking, of which the paradigm is Kant's epistemological rescue of the truth element in metaphysics (discussed in chapter 4). This mode of thinking, cultivated by both Kant and Adorno, could be called, in today's terminology, a "weak concept of metaphysics." In light of the contemporary theory of knowledge, materialist critique, and modern philosophy of science, any metaphysics that still laid claim to the status of ontology or theology would be obsolete. Adorno's "negative metaphysics," however, no longer claims to define "the essence of the human"—as though one could do so from a quasi-divine perspective, independent of our limited abilities to make statements on the matter and independent of cultural and historical changes in our concept of the human. This skepticism about metaphysics applies not only to definitions of the human. Adorno's concept of the nonidentical reminds us "that things are not exhausted by what is known about them," something Kant already understood.[7]

Those arguments concern metaphysics as the science of making distinctions. But even the classical, affirmative metaphysics of permanent and unchanging essences appeared to Adorno in a new light. The practical consequence of the abstract negation of traditional metaphysics was, he argued, the expropriation of the one remaining thing human beings in the death camps might have experienced as their own: their own deaths. This expropriation occurred when human beings no longer died as individuals, but were instead degraded and extinguished as numbers.

In Adorno's view, metaphysical experience is essentially the expectation of happiness. It is invariably disappointed, as one learns from Marcel Proust. But it is the foundation for an internal model of happiness, for a critical measurement of what happens to the subject in actuality, for what the subject can actually achieve in the here and now. Here, again, Adorno thinks dualistically: the "potential" in the dimension of metaphysical experience is juxtaposed with what is actually the case. Adorno speaks of the "surplus beyond the subject . . . which subjective metaphysical experience refuses to give up." He stresses that we cannot hold "in our hands" what metaphysical experience merely "suggests" to us. But metaphysical experience is sustained by a negative relation to life. An example of this negative relation appears in Beckett's *Endgame*, in the question "Is that everything?" which, Adorno writes, "becomes actual through the futility of waiting." The expectations nourished by metaphysics are not guaranteed by any certainty: "Futile waiting does not guarantee the reality of what is being waited for, but reflects the condition measured by what has failed." The metaphor of reflection indicates how important the motif of dualism is for Adorno. The abstract negation of the foundations of metaphysical cognition entails a loss of ability to differentiate. It would be false to pursue affirmative metaphysics and start from changeless, eternal essences, but just as false to squander the epistemological gain brought by the initiation of a negative metaphysics.

6

The Goal of
the Emancipated Society

A "JUST" SUBLIMATION of the principle of individuation within a free society is, for Adorno, thoroughly imaginable. If, in bourgeois society, the individual is constituted by the principle of economic production, emerging as its substratum and becoming indispensable to it, then, in the totally socialized society transformed into an authoritarian state, the individual is abstractly negated. In the post-totalitarian society, the economic basis of which is the capitalist economic structure becoming comparably totalized, the individual celebrates its apparent resurrection. But what might an existence look like that had overcome the authoritarian imagery of individuation, which is fixated on productivity and denotes the end of actual individuals? What might an "undamaged life" be, a condition "in which life could be lived without fear"?

Adorno gives us no detailed picture of utopia. He refuses to conjure up images of the better condition. He stresses that the Old Testament prohibition on images remains philosophically and socially mandatory—in an explicitly transformed sense, to be sure: not as a taboo, but as a requirement of intellectual self-discipline, designed to protect thought against measuring "the wholly different" by the standards of what is. If, as stated at the outset, the objective goal of negation is something better—that is, to produce something positive, even if it cannot yet be named and given concrete form—then it must be possible to define its essence conceptually. Adorno's critique does have a standard: it is the "idea . . . of a fulfilled humanity." Only on this basis can he define precisely the "objective blocking-off of what is better," which he discusses frequently. This permits him to formulate conclusions—or rather anticipations—about what is being blocked off. Ernst Bloch and Adorno, normally irreconcilable opposites in utopian matters, were able, in a 1964 radio conversation, to converse agreeably on this central point: "Teddy, I think we agree about this: utopia's essential function is to critique what actually is. But if we had not crossed the limits, we could not even recognize them as limits." To these words of Bloch, Adorno responds, "Yes, utopia is fundamentally concealed in the defined negation of what actually is, which, since it becomes concretely present as something false, always simultaneously reminds us of what should be." Thus, for Adorno, the utopia of a just society can be reached only through a detour, in fact a double detour: both via the critique of existing society and via the critique of the most progressive counterimage to that society. The aphorism "Sur l'eau" [On the Water] from *Minima Moralia* is devoted to this problem:

> To the question about the goal of emancipated society, one receives answers such as the fulfillment of human possibilities or life's richness. If the unavoidable question is illegitimate, then equally inevitable is the repulsive self-promotion of the answer, evoking the memory of the social-democratic ideal of personality advanced by the full-bearded naturalists of the 1890s, seeking to live life to the fullest. Only the crudest point has the necessary gentleness: that henceforth no one should go hungry. Everything else posits a condition to be defined by human needs, using a model of human behavior shaped by the axiom of production as an end in itself.

Posing questions about the goals of a just society is illegitimate because projecting forward from the perspective of existing conditions can generate only false answers. Yet asking these questions is inescapable, because, in an analogy to Marx's observation that the ape's anatomy can be rendered accessible only through that of the human being, a critique of existing society is only possible within the horizon of a different, realizable world. As Adorno puts it, "The existing world can be grasped only by someone concerned, above all, about a possible, better world." The goal proclaimed by the revolutionary social movements was the realization of what should have been possible and achievable for human beings in this century, on the basis of already manifest social productivity: namely, a life that guaranteed material and spiritual wealth to all, thereby fulfilling the potential of the human species. But Adorno views this "positive" formula as an unconscious variation on the bourgeois ideal of productivity and achievement. In Adorno's view, a genuinely free society would be possible only through liberation from the established law of profit-oriented production of goods.

In one of his last writings, Adorno stresses, using Marxist concepts, "that contemporary society, based on industrial labor, is indeed an 'industrial' society oriented exclusively toward the condition of its forces of production. . . . Society simply is capitalism in its relations of production. Human beings still are what they were according to Marx's mid-nineteenth-century analysis: appendages of the machinery." Industrial society affects "no longer just literally the workers who have to structure their lives according to the machines they are servicing." Rather, today all human beings "are required metaphorically, to a far greater extent, to insert themselves in the social machine with specific roles to play, and to model themselves accordingly, without reservation. Today, as before, production is engaged in exclusively for profit. To an extent far greater than what was imaginable in Marx's time, human needs have become, as was always a possibility, completely identified as functions of the apparatus of production, not vice versa. They are totally regulated." We cannot predict how human needs would be shaped in a society where people were no longer appendages of the apparatus of production, but Adorno is certain these needs would not be contained in concepts such as fulfillment or wealth. In the 1940s he writes, both aggressively and dialectically, that in a society liberated from the "persistence of class rule, human need will appear completely different. . . . If production is immediately, wholly and unconditionally reordered toward the satisfaction of needs, including and especially those generated by capitalism, then in that very process the needs themselves will change decisively." We cannot specify exactly how these needs would change, but we can precisely define the design fault built into the vision of fulfillment expressed in the tradition of utopian socialism. As Adorno later summarizes in *Negative Dialectics*, "the concept of a full life, including the one promised to human beings by socialist conceptions, is precisely not the utopia it misjudges itself to be, because that fullness cannot be separated from greed, from what the *Jugendstil* termed living life to the fullest, from a longing that contains both violence and subjugation."

In the aphorism "Sur l'eau" the error of affirmative utopia is discernible above all in the fact that three core elements of bourgeois society are hypostasized: the fetish character of the commodity, the concept of dynamism, and the concept of nature. Adorno continues,

> Into the desired image of the unrestrained, defiant, creative human being has trickled the fetishism of the commodity which, in bourgeois society, brings with it inhibition, impotence, the sterility of eternal repetition. The concept of dynamism, a key complementary element of bourgeois "ahistoricity," is elevated to the status of an absolute—whereas, as an anthropological reflex of the laws of production, it would necessarily, in an emancipated society, have to be confronted critically with the actuality of need. The image of untrammeled action, of incessant creativity, of innocent insatiability, of freedom as being ceaselessly busy—this image feeds off that bourgeois concept of nature, which has from the start been suited exclusively for proclaiming social violence as inevitable, as an element of healthy eternity. For this reason, not because of the official goal of equality, the positive imaginings of socialism, which Marx resisted, remained mired in barbarism. It is not humanity growing slack in prosperity that is to be feared, but the chaotic expansion of the social dynamic disguised as universal nature, collectivity as a blind rage of activity.

According to Marx, in the advanced capitalist exchange economy, the social character of human products appears as an inherently natural quality. Marx calls this state of affairs "fetishism of the commodity and its secret," and his explanation of it plays a central role in his critique of political economy. A commodity is formally defined by its exchange value, which is measured by the quantum of socially necessary labor time stored within it. Exchange value places everything in a specific relation to every other thing. Yet the criteria according to which we exchange things as commodities appear to emanate from the things themselves. As Kurt Lenk summarizes,

> In the capitalist commodity society, the process of production and reproduction of material life has become independent of the actual needs of human beings. In the exchange process, human products become self-sufficient entities, objects of value that seem to possess an autonomous dynamic independent of human activity. The laws of the anonymous market are manifest as blind, inexorable powers, behind which social power relations are fundamentally concealed. All goods circulating in the capitalist marketplace cease to be tangible concrete objects and ossify into commodities. Their formal value is perceived not as an expression of social relations, but as a quality inherent in the objects themselves. By analogy to this fetishizing of the commodity world, the products of human thought are objectified as autonomous forces that appear to guide history.

The principle of Marx's critique of ideology is expressed in the demystifying of the fetish character of the commodity, which was developed further in the critical Marxism of Georg Lukács and Karl Korsch. In Lukács's epochal work, *History and Class Consciousness*, the concept of objectification became a key component of critical theory, albeit in modified form. Critical theory shares the diagnosis with Lukács. Impotence, obstruction of individual and collective possibilities, as well as the aridity of a seemingly strict codification of productive life—which is actually occurring—result from the social structuring of commodity exchange because, in Lukács's words, "a relationship between people acquires a thinglike character and consequently a 'ghostly objectivity' which, in its strict, seemingly closed and rational inherent laws, covers up all traces of its essence, namely, actual human relations." But in Lukács's view the diagnosis is simultaneously the cure: the phenomenon of objectification, insofar as it affects the proletariat, becomes, as if by dialectical magic, the driving factor in the formation of revolutionary class consciousness, which necessarily leads to the overcoming of objectification.[1] Here the critical minds diverge. Adorno argues, in *Negative Dialectics*, "Dialectics are no more reducible to objectification than to any other isolated category." And their systemic difference of opinion is supplemented by a difference in social-historical experience. Detached from its original critical context, the concept of objectification has become a subjectivist, pseudocritical term under which one can categorize all manner of undesirable things: "The lament about objectification meanwhile slides over the reality of human suffering rather than denouncing it. The true disaster lies in the social relations that condemn people to impotence and apathy, but which they actually could change, not primarily in the people themselves and their perception of these relations." Finally, Adorno adds another dimension: it is no longer the antagonism between classes but the inner antagonism of the social totality, in the form of the violent self-extinction of the human essence, that is now social-theoretically decisive: "In face of the possibility of total catastrophe, objectification is an epiphenomenon; what counts is the mental alienation that goes with it, the subjective condition resulting from it."

Adorno contends, in the aphorism "Sur l'eau," that even attempts to escape the bourgeois imperatives of productivity and commerce remain trapped within them, because it is virtually impossible even to imagine a fundamentally different principle of socialization. The attempts to break out of the self-built cage suffer, in their fixation on wealth and affluence, from the fact that the laws of the cage's construction appear to be unchangeable laws of nature. The same goes for the revolutionary impetus of a supposedly comprehensively developed personality, behind which, in Adorno's view, there is nothing more than the primal bourgeois topos: dynamism of the progressive, rational domination of nature. As Adorno stresses, writing in the early 1960s in dialogue with the classic German sociologies by Max Weber and Werner Sombart, traditional feudal societies are succeeded, in the modern era, by societies characterized by bourgeois rationality. However, this rationality is the ahistorical type defined by the universal exchange principle; hence, as was already pointed out in *Dialectic of Enlightenment,* this rationality tends inherently toward its opposite, irrationality. The bartering process unleashes a dynamic of progressive development of productive forces. However, this dynamic remains in thrall to the static structure of the relations of production that have remained unchanged in the present, i.e., they remain ultimately relations of ownership. Abstraction from all qualitative, mutually incommensurable definitions of object and individuals—essential, in Marx's analysis, for the process of exchange—leads, in Adorno's view, first to the elimination of memory and second to the fundamental paralysis of the dynamic modern society, just as the stress on aesthetic novelty generates the ghostly recurrence of what is forever the same:

> The established antithesis between feudal traditionalism and radical bourgeois society, of private and public memory as an irrational burden in the wake of the progressive rationalization of industrial modes of production; these industrializing processes reduce not only vestiges of the craftsman's skills but also categories such as periods of apprenticeship, the essence of cumulative experience—which, however, is hardly necessary any more. If humanity, in its present phase, renounces memory in order to exhaust itself in its breathless adaptation to whatever is current, this process reflects an objective developmental structure. Just as stasis is the social premise of dynamism, so the dynamism of progressive, rational domination of nature culminates teleologically in stasis. The graveyard peace of totalitarianism—enemy of true peace—reveals, as excessive dominance of the oppressors over the oppressed, that rationality becomes real only for the minority. Blind domination of nature, swallowing it up as if it were an enemy, remains inherently hostile, attuned to the primal antagonism between rulers and slaves.

The bourgeois concept of nature, of which Adorno speaks in *Minima Moralia*, collapses the distinction between nature and its other, rationality, by quantifying nature, thus making it controllable. As Max Weber says, the world is demystified by science and technology. But at the same time, as Horkheimer and Adorno note, the world is endowed with a new spell. Nature is repressed, only to return compulsively. Social institutions, and above all relations of power and property, turn into relations seemingly inherent in nature, frozen into objectivity. They appear to be a second nature. As Adorno writes in *Dialectic of Enlightenment*, "Civilization is the triumph of society over nature, turning everything into mere nature. Yet society perpetuates the threat of nature as the enduring, organized compulsion which, reproducing itself in individuals as the logic of self-preservation, retaliates against nature in the form of social domination over it." To break out of this circle should be the goal of self-consciously liberating praxis and would involve renouncing all existing forms of praxis. Only actions of solidarity by the human race, focused on creating peace with the nature both inside and outside ourselves, could, in Adorno's view, be a position to renounce the quantifying subjection of everything individual under the general law of bourgeois economics that has today become totalizing; only then could other forms of human self-reproduction be imagined.

In this context, Adorno anticipates motifs of an ecologically conscious relation to nature, which today, more than ever, are in a position to claim validity. As Adorno writes in the aphorism "Sur l'eau,"

> The naively assumed uniformity in the developmental tendency toward increased production is itself a product of that bourgeois atmosphere which allows only a single developmental direction because, as a closed totality, it is ruled by quantification and hostile to qualitative difference. . . . If one thinks of the emancipated society as an emancipation from precisely that totality, vanishing lines become visible that have little in common with the increase in production and its human mirrorings. If unrestrained human beings are by no means the most agreeable and not even the freest, then conversely the society with its shackles removed could recall that productive powers do not convey the human being's ultimate essence, but only the form historically designed for the production of commodities. Perhaps a true society will grow tired of development and, for the sake of freedom, leave possibilities unexploited, instead of invading strange planets, driven by a crazy compulsion.

The unrestrained behavior of our technical-industrial complex toward the nature surrounding us is responsible for our inability to control rationally the metabolic processes of our relation with nature. This inability has produced a situation in which collective extinction, through our own destruction of the organic basis of life, no longer appears unthinkable. Restraint in a double sense, namely, moderation in relation to nature and control of the economic mechanisms that lead to its devastation, has become vital to life itself. This kind of restraint is completely other than the one Adorno refers to when he deems it a result of the fetishism of commodities in bourgeois society. The latter type of restraint is a psychological blockade of unrestrained, self-defining reason through the pressures of commodity production. This "restraint" produces the total lack of restraint of blind expansion and subjective extravagance. The counterpart to this lack of restraint would be a careful withdrawal from subjective extravagance, a self-conscious reduction of human productive energies. Today, it is no longer a secret that restraining the self's needs in its interaction with external nature is urgently necessary. We are constantly reminded of that necessity in public and political ecological discourse. But so far the core insight has remained without consequences. And one could say that Adorno anticipated both the insight that is fully actual fifty years later as well as the reason it is blocked from being effective: society's lack of autonomy, which persists despite the political declarations and resolutions—all without results—announcing the goal of a reflective, careful, "restrained" relation with nature.

There is another issue, urgently relevant today, for which Adorno's critical theory offers an implicit road map. The ecological discourse normally argues for the preservation of nature, often conceptualized as "first nature." But this concept does not do justice to the problem. For if one acknowledges that the nature with which we are presently engaged is always already "a social and historical production of mankind," then the dogma of preservation is shown to be deceptive, because it masks the fact that we have never *not* intervened in nature's systems. A better goal would be the humane shaping of nature, which would organize human interventions through the possibilities of successful living within nature's order. The social formation of nature and the dialectical connection between internal and external nature are two motifs which are treated paradigmatically in *Dialectic of Enlightenment*.

The economics of today's society are those of an ever more global capitalist barter society; its increasingly crisis-prone, contradictory productivity is rooted in the fact that, for individuals, innovative personal risks, experiences, and media sensations are constantly becoming available. These new experiences, however, are not really new, but only variations within a prescribed bandwidth. Adorno's conceptual image of a just society looks bucolic by contrast: the satisfaction of individual needs, freedom from incessant productivity growth, and freedom to interact gently with a nature that is experienced as one's own being within the other. To be sure, these ideals are articulated not as affirmative utopian pastoral idyll but in the strict modality of the defined negation of existing structures. From the negation of the abstract cult of progress there follows compellingly, for Adorno, the linkage to an enlightened core idea within Kant's philosophy. In Adorno's view, a just society would cancel both the stasis and the dynamism of bourgeois society. As he writes in the 1960s, "It would neither contain merely existent structures that bind human beings for the sake of an order that would no longer need such shackles, as soon as it became at one with humanity's interests; nor would it continue to drive the blind momentum, that antithesis of the eternal peace which is for Kant the goal of history." This view returns to an idea already noted by Adorno in "Sur l'eau": there he outlines very concretely what could result from defined negation of bourgeois dynamics. He conjures up a materialist vision of a naturalness at peace, released from constraint.

> A humanity that no longer endures need begins to understand something of the illusory, pointless quality of all the arrangements hitherto undertaken to escape need, which reproduced need as well as wealth on a larger scale. Humanity's pleasure is affected by this awareness, as is the inseparability of its current life pattern from hectic activity, planning, imposing one's will and subjugation. *Rien faire comme une bête*, lying on the water and gazing peacefully at the sky, "simply exist-

ing, without any other mission or fulfillment"—such living could replace the structures of doing, striving and fulfilling, thereby truly redeeming the promise of dialectical logic to end where it began. No abstract concept comes closer to a fulfilled utopia than that of eternal peace.

The title of Adorno's aphorism "Sur l'eau" is also the title of a story by Guy de Maupassant, an author esteemed by Adorno. But Maupassant's story does not, as one might assume, tell of a happy person lying on the water in blissful idleness, peacefully contemplating the sky. Instead, Maupassant describes an oppressive scenario: while sailing at night a man casts the anchor in order to take a breather in the good weather and peaceful moonlight. Yet he is soon overcome by an inexplicable anxiety. He would like to start moving again, but detects at once that something binds his anchor to the riverbed. As impenetrable fog suddenly begins to rise, the boatman is trapped for the night in the middle of the river, fearful and incapable of making his boat move. His fear intensifies into a "terrified panic," which he controls only with difficulty. Finally, the fog lifts from the river. The boatman ceases to be fearful; he feels suddenly enchanted by the nocturnal landscape. In the morning a fisherman comes to his aid. They discover why the boat was immobilized: underwater the anchor had been caught in the corpse of an old woman with a "large stone attached to her neck."

It is puzzling that Adorno would appropriate Maupassant's dark story for his speculation concerning the just society and the false present. Surely it is not a literary image of a better condition. Perhaps Maupassant's story is an allegory of the aporia of progress in bourgeois society; like the man in the boat, we never get anywhere because, while we are able to dominate nature, we remain trapped in the hidden context of destructive violence, which we long to escape. So long as we fail in this, we cannot lie on the water peacefully, but only in panic and under threat. The peace that we sometimes experience, enchantment by natural beauty, is illusory, so long as the world is organized in such a way that human beings must commit suicide and, from below, hold the living in their spell.[2]

Like Walter Benjamin, Adorno is convinced that it is not the continued, unthinking, technological domination of nature, but only the "control of the relation between nature and humanity," grounded in solidarity, that can begin to liberate human beings from their prehistory. In *One-Way Street*, Benjamin expressed the hope that a self-aware proletariat would create, in a "creative rush," humanity's "new body"; Adorno, by contrast, still sees in such visions of creativity traces of bourgeois productive thinking. In place of productivity, activity, and procedural structures, Benjamin's vision has contemplation, peace, and being. Hence Adorno's ironic engagement with Hegel's logic.

In Hegel's logic, the very definition of the theory of being contains the basic procedural model of speculative dialectics. The core logical concepts are not fixed and rigid, but structured through internal contradiction. That is why they ceaselessly generate counter-concepts from their inner core. For Hegel, the logical structure of thinking lies in the projection of the dialectical unity between conceptual identity and difference. Logic's first core concept is being. But "being, pure being, without any further definition" produces nothing as a core concept. "In its undefined immediacy," pure being is abstract, empty being—hence void, indistinguishable from nothingness. To that extent, the concept of being already contains its opposite, the concept of nothingness, within itself. The transition from being to nothingness is becoming. Becoming is "the movement of unmediated dissolution of the one concept in the other." Being, nothingness, and becoming are, in the dialectical organization of core logical categories, thesis, antithesis, and synthesis. To put it in terms of content: in being, as such, there is already the process, the transition, the ceaseless progression of the idea—and hence, according to Hegel, the idea of the thing in itself. Hegel's logic posits that the movement of mind ultimately merges with itself when the restless self-production of the idea or of the concept culminates again in being, only to renounce itself once again and to pursue, in a renewed progression, the perpetual circular movement.

Adorno deploys this model of the philosophy of history ironically. According to this model, happy, animal idleness is the telos of the unceasing labor of the human species; flowing into one's origin is the fulfilled homecoming. For Adorno, this homecoming converges with the goal of "eternal peace." With this phrase Kant projects a conception of the rights of states and peoples that would be in a position to overcome humanity's warlike primal nature through a permanent actualization of morality. For Kant, this achievement is politically possible only in a federally structured world citizenship. The peaceful overcoming of human hostility and state-organized antagonisms can be imagined only through the "positive idea of a world republic." For the time being, Kant sees this idea as embodied in real history by "the negative surrogate of an existing, ever-growing league committed to opposing war." Adorno reinterprets this motif in "Sur l'eau." For him peace is not only, as it is for Kant, "the end of all hostilities," but also defined positively as freedom, pleasure, and contemplation. Within the abstract concept of eternal peace is concealed an "intention" directed toward a fulfilled utopia.

"However little we are in a position to portray utopia," says Adorno in the radio conversation with Bloch,

> however unsure we are of what would be truly just, to that same extent we know for sure what is truly wrong. That is really the only form in which the idea of justice is given to us. But I still do believe—Ernst, perhaps we should discuss this—that this question remains very complex since, just because we're forbidden to generate positive images, something very bad happens: the more it becomes possible only to talk negatively about what should be, the less one is able to imagine anything definite about it. But then—and this is probably more disturbing still—this prohibition on concrete statements about utopia tends to denigrate utopian consciousness as such and to block what is really important, namely, the will to transform. . . . If it is true that a free and happy life would be possible today, then one theoretical form of utopia would involve saying concretely what would be possible given the current status of humanity's productive powers: this really can be said, without embellishment or arbitrariness. If it is not said, if this vision does not appear, I almost want to say *tangibly*, then basically one does not know what the point of it all is, why the whole mental apparatus is being set in motion. Forgive me if I adopt the unexpected viewpoint of the positivist, but I believe that without this factor a phenomenology of utopian consciousness would be just impossible.

Adorno indulged in no false hopes about the scope of utopian consciousness. He would not have been surprised at the extent to which it is denigrated nowadays. "That freedom remained primarily an ideology; that human beings are powerless in relation to the system and unable to define, on the basis of reason, their own life and that of society as a whole; indeed, that they can no longer even think about that without increasing their suffering—all this gives their rebellious instinct a completely false character: maliciously, they prefer what is worse to the appearance of something better." Not only is this psychological state anchored in subjectivity, but for Adorno it also gives, in a weird way, expression to an objective condition. The "ever-present terror" that threatens us is the fever of a society that has become totally rigid and "threatened by total destruction."

The Powerless Utopia of Beauty

IF THE PRINCIPLE OF CEASELESS PRODUCTIVITY and its intensification were ended without violence, then there could also be a change in the character of that productive process which in present-day society serves other goals than the making of commodities. By this is meant the production of art. As Adorno writes in *Aesthetic Theory*:

> Works of art are the placeholders of things no longer disfigured by the barter process, of that which is not injured by the profit motive and the false needs of a devalued humanity. . . . A free society would be liberated from the means-ends rationality of exploitation. That is encoded in art and is its explosive social potential.

For "art has, within the prevailing utilitarian orthodoxy, an authentically utopian quality"; it directs attention to "the other, that which is exempt from the hustle of society's productive and reproductive process, is not subject to the reality principle." Yet making art is very hard work. The lives of Kafka, Proust, Flaubert, and van Gogh were completely other than what is conjured up by the image of lying happily by the water; to think of them is to realize how painful and tormenting the production of art can be.

Art does not have for Adorno, as it does for Bloch, the status of a "preview" of what human beings have been able to imagine, in their given historical situation, as elements of a just society. While assigning a utopian character to art, Adorno sees it as profoundly contradictory:

> Among today's antinomies a central one is that art must be utopia and wishes it so—indeed the more decisively so, the more its real-life functional context obstructs any vision of utopia; yet at the same time art may not actually be utopia, in order not to betray it as illusion and consolation. If art's utopia were to be realized, that would be the historical end of art. Hegel was the first to see this as implicit in its very concept.

Hegel's prognosis of the "end of art" has not yet been fulfilled. (We will leave it as an open question whether it really was a prognosis, in the sense Adorno attributes to Hegel. It was Hegel's intention to demonstrate that art, in his own historical moment, had surrendered to scientifically reflective philosophy its formerly justified claim to be the highest form of understanding. Adorno understood this way of thinking in an even more historically self-conscious form than Hegel did. He dramatizes the motif of the "end of art" within the framework of his theory of the end of culture in the culture industry.) Adorno leaves open the possibility that the end of art might yet come to pass, but in two completely opposite ways. He distinguishes between the tendency to a false cancellation of art as an "unreflective, in a repulsive sense realistic affirmation and duplication of things as they are"—and the perhaps utopian, at the very least counterfactual, perspective of a just, conciliatory overcoming of art actualized by the satisfaction of the needs that motivate the production of art. It is entirely conceivable for Adorno that, in a rationally structured society liberated from publicly generated suffering, art might disappear altogether, rather than eking out a particularist existence based on the division of labor. In the 1940s he was still certain of it. As he unambiguously states in

The Philosophy of Modern Music, "Art would die only for a humanity at peace; the death of art that threatens today would be solely the triumph of mere existence over the gaze of a consciousness that fails to stand up to it." Later, Adorno's prognosis became more cautious when he speculated about the peaceful "dying" of art in a society liberated from antagonisms. Why, even in such a utopian condition, should art end? Could it not perhaps authentically begin then? As he puts it in *Aesthetic Theory*, "It is possible that a peaceful society would be open to an art of the past that today has become the ideological counterweight of nonpeaceful society." The passage reads like an answer to his thinking in *The Philosophy of Modern Music*. He continues:

> That the newly emergent art might return to peace and order, to affirmative imagery and harmony, would entail the sacrifice of its expressive freedom. It is inappropriate even to project the shape of art in a transformed society. It would probably be completely other than past and present art, but it would be more desirable that, in a better time, art should disappear altogether, than that it should forget the suffering it expresses and which gives substance to its form.

If we were free from suffering, perhaps we would no longer need an aesthetically shaped memory. But would we, in a society liberated from the antagonisms of economics and domination, also be free from suffering? Would we then no longer need the solidarity of remembering past suffering? Such considerations shape Adorno's reservations when he speculates on a "successful" end of art. Thoughts about a "false" end have priority in his mind.

The Destruction and Salvation of Art

Minima Moralia also contains thoughts about the end of art. As Adorno argues, only the "destruction of art" can be "its salvation." But what "destruction" does he mean? Against the background of the actual world-historical experience underlying *Minima Moralia*, one might assume that the issue was the destruction closing in not only on art but also on life itself. The destruction that took place in the

Second World War was even more catastrophic than than that of the First. For Adorno, the First World War's destructions found convincing expression in Stravinsky's *Soldier's Tale*, in that compressed score for "chamber group battered by shocks" whose "dreamlike compulsiveness" simultaneously expressed real and ideational destruction. Indeed, it is a core assumption of Adorno's aesthetic that art is committed to the formal working through of the experience of suffering, the essence of which is always historical and, in the most recent times, catastrophic. Adorno's aesthetics are surely modernist, since, in his view, it is nineteenth-century works of art, such as those of Vincent van Gogh, for example, that "rage with the storm of all the emotions that, for the first time, the individual of his era registered as the catastrophe of history." But now Adorno is concerned with something different, with what could be called the symbolic destruction of art—or, more precisely, the symbolic self-destruction of art.

"De gustibus est disputandum" [It is essential to argue about taste] is the title of this aphorism in *Minima Moralia*. It is not only possible to argue about taste, it is essential to do so, because aesthetics are involved with truth, indeed with an objective claim to truth. For Kant, the aesthetic judgment of taste is marked by a characteristic ambivalence. It cannot do otherwise than make a claim to truth and to general validity, yet at the same time it is not in a position to formulate objective, universalizing arguments for this claim. "A beautiful object gives general pleasure without abstract justification," Kant writes, and further "is acknowledged as an indisputable source of pleasure." The claim to universal validity cannot be rigorously redeemed, but it is inseparable from aesthetic judgment. It is, so to speak, the drive of aesthetic judgment toward truth—going beyond itself and beyond what it can contain in its own realm—that cannot be stabilized conceptually. If we let go of this problematic dimension by withdrawing into the closed circle of nonbinding aesthetic subjectivism, refusing rational discussion—discussion with arguments—concerning judgments of taste, then we keep "the reflection on truth and the claim to it at a distance from works of art." To Adorno, that is precisely what seems appropriate for today's "solid bourgeoisie, for whom art can never be irrational enough." But the result is not what today's apologists may have in mind when they advocate "anything goes"—a phrase still gently ironic in Cole Porter's usage, which has now become serious dogma—the concept-free pseudopluralism, in which anyone can do as he pleases, rejecting with irritation the question about an artwork's authenticity as philosophical pretentiousness. This pluralism does not generate the desired, supposedly varied multiplicity of "the incomparability of works of art." Rather, it produces the bad infinity of artistic randomness, which is the mortal enemy of works of art, because it simply ignores their immanent claim to be taken seriously and evaluated accordingly. This claim is inherent in the seriousness with which artworks make it. In Adorno's view, artworks evaluate both their extra-aesthetic reality and, at least implicitly, all other artworks. They cannot coexist peacefully. Every work of art wants to stand up for its entire truth claim, Adorno argues from a Hegelian perspective. And art's truth claim is the mortal enemy of indifferent aesthetic relativism, itself structured by commodified consciousness. Today, in the form of eclecticism, targeted also by Lyotard, relativism has become the dominant form of aesthetic false consciousness. Yet in the aphorism "De gustibus est disputandum" the issue is not eclecticism but, rather, the genuine end of art: its destruction which is simultaneously to be its salvation. Adorno thinks of it as "true beauty free of all appearance."

Appearance-free beauty: that sounds like a paradox, even a small self-contradiction, but is not so for an idealist metaphysics of essence. The medium of art, and of the beauty that traditionally defines it, is appearance. In traditional metaphysics, appearance is the opposite of being, the locus of deception and illusion about what is real. Philosophy, understood as the doctrine of being, seeks to know what is real. It can do so only by penetrating what appears to be real but in truth is not. It thereby seizes hold of being itself, of the essence that is present behind ceaselessly shifting appearances, behind the process of becoming. Essence does not become real, then disappear, but is eternal and unchanging, antithetical to appearance, which cannot be comprehended but only experienced. Experience cannot generate knowledge, only opinion. In Plato's view, the appearance of beauty hides the idea of beauty. The idea is divine and can be reached only by setting aside appearance, which belongs to the realm of the natural and ephemeral.

In the realm of ideas, beauty without appearance can exist, because the *idea* of beauty does not only appear, but actually is. Traditional metaphysics sought to discern the essence of three ideas: truth, beauty, and goodness. In the classicism of the bourgeoisie, these ideas reemerge as governing concepts, falsified into ideology, in order to embody the bourgeois ideal of *Bildung* (cultivation), as in the motto carved into the front of the Frankfurt Opera. Adorno bade farewell to these standards as social untruth, though not without a certain melancholy, when talking with Kracauer in the 1920s in the Westend Café. That does not mean, of course, that Adorno thereby rejected the truth claim of classical philosophy. In "Plato's hypostasizing of the concept into the idea," which is then raised to absolute status, is contained "the untruth of the doctrine of self-sufficient truth." Yet the role of the absolute in critical theory is retained as a negating concept, as the other of the existing situation. If philosophy simply discards the thought of the absolute—and Horkheimer and Adorno see modern thinking as doing just that—then any kind of distancing from the existing situation is degraded into mere fiction, into subjective fantasy. Critique, which for Adorno is based fundamentally in a virtual distancing from things as they are, is thereby systematically rendered impossible.

> Philosophy, being after everything solely responsible for its situation, could no longer think itself capable of postulating the absolute, indeed had to prohibit the very thought to itself, in order not to betray that thought; yet it could not allow the emphatic concept of truth to be devalued in any way. This contradiction pervades contemporary philosophy, rendering its negativity inescapable.

Returning to aesthetics and the issue of the dignity of the category of appearance: only in modern times does idealist philosophy glimpse the possibility that sensuous cognition can be justified as a different but authentic mode of knowledge. The gradual rehabilitation of appearance begins with Baumgarten's theorization of aesthetics as a doctrine of nonconceptual knowledge.[1] Finally, Hegel demonstrates the immanent contradiction of a spiritual metaphysics that neglects the dialectic between essence and appearance. According to Hegel, "appearance itself is essential to essence; truth would not exist if it did not manifest itself in appearance." Because "beauty has its life in appearance," philosophical aesthetics must be acknowledged and validated as an indispensable form of the experience of truth which, in its otherness that is not genuinely conceptual, nevertheless has a conceptual core.

Plato's metaphysics of ideas, in its Parmenidean stasis, imagines beauty without appearance. Hegel's metaphysics of spirit, in its Heraclitean dynamism, demonstrates dialectically the impossibility of this conception. But it does not thereby rescue the genuine character of appearance; rather, it delivers it even more persistently to be subsumed under the spiritual content that in Hegel's system is the substance of all that is, the substance of totality. The important thing for Adorno cannot be beauty without appearance as an idealist construct, nor can it be rescuing appearance by demonstrating its ideal substance. Adorno perceives in the truth content of aesthetic appearance a differently shaped tendency toward transcending appearance.

Even Hegel assigns only ephemeral status to the truth of art. He understands it as a stage that the spirit reaches, passes through, then abandons again, in order to attain higher versions of itself: religion and philosophy. Adorno, however, understands the concept of self-transcendence not idealistically but as a way of reaching the core element of all art which, following Stendhal and Baudelaire, he recognizes in the identification of beauty with a "promise of happiness." This identification implies a way of negatively aiming at a condition where the aesthetic promise of happiness would no longer be needed, since beauty and happiness would no longer be mere appearances but actual reality. "Stendhal's dictum of the *promesse du bonheur* says that art expresses gratitude to existence by foregrounding the elements that anticipate utopia," Adorno writes. Adorno therefore defines art as "an allegory of unmediated happiness beyond appearance," encumbered "with the mortal proviso of the chimerical: that it does not exist." The self-manifesting of the artwork points toward a happiness that could not only appear in the world but also embody its existent truth. Art is not deceptive per se, for it is not in league with the fact that happiness does not exist but, rather, embodies its very possibility. "The existence of artworks testifies to the possibility of the possible." However, art can be the placeholder of the other only in the paradoxically ruptured mode of seeming to recall or be mindful of what has never been. The model of this process, for Adorno, is Proust's quest for a past that suddenly appears to the remembering subject, which is wholly constituted by memory work and thus is at once appropriated by memory and lost to it. "The longing at the core of artworks—for the reality of that which is not—is transformed by them into memory. In memory that which is, once past, can be fused with what is not, since the past no longer is." The locus of the dream "of what not yet is" is the "act of recall that alone can make utopia concrete, without betraying it to what actually is. That which is is inseparable from appearance: even in the past it was not real per se."

If motifs from Kant's aesthetics enter, transformed, into Adorno's materialist version of the idea of the end of art, this is no relapse into pre-Hegelian discourse. Rather, it is the necessary tribute that materialist thinking must pay to objectivity, the priority of which Adorno asserts, in *Negative Dialectics*, is central to his program of utopian cognition. This tribute is due once Hegel's dissolution of everything nonconceptual in objects of thought, in favor of their idealistically assumed spiritual structure, is recognized in its totality as false consciousness. Kant stresses that the logic of aesthetic form cannot be presumed a priori, but only induced a posteriori, through abstraction from the individual work. Any prescriptive aesthetics would therefore be alien to art's actuality. When Kant writes that "the rule must be induced from the deed, that is, from what is actually produced," he directs philosophical aesthetics toward the works themselves as its primary material. Adorno, who at least contemplates "the possibility of an aesthetic doctrine of form that is both comprehensive and material," without claiming that he could realize it, agrees with Kant on this point. But like Hegel, Adorno envisages the development, the unfolding of aesthetic productivity, and hence what is permitted, necessary, or forbidden in the production of art, from the perspective of art's objective reality. Like Hegel, he thinks within the framework of an aesthetics grounded in the philosophy of history.

But this difference from Kant is only one aspect of Adorno's aesthetics. One element they have in common is the doctrine of the priority in aesthetics of the object, of the specific work. In Kant this idea is very limited, because in general he argues for an aesthetics of taste and reception, focused on the responses of the subject. Adorno, by contrast, analyzes the objective experiential content that works of art substantially embody, in part spiritually, in part mimetically. He shares this approach with Hegel. For Adorno, works of art express one of several responses of the human mind to objectivity. The dialectic of mimesis and rationality defines not only the reception and production of works, but also their truth content. Works of art are simultaneously experience and cognition—in a sense that, to be sure, differs with every work. In science and philosophy, there is a basic level of sedimented experience that never quite dissolves into the dimension of conceptual structure, but very likely affects it by osmosis. Similarly, Adorno sees in even the most hermetically subjective and monadic work of art a basic level of rationality, expressed in the fact that the work either obeys a constructive logic or functions in a tension-ridden relation to that logic.

> Art is a mimetic performance that has at its disposal, for its self-objectification, the most advanced forms of rationality with which to shape its material and procedures. This contradiction corresponds to that of reason itself. If reason's telos could be termed a fulfillment that is not necessarily rational per se—happiness is the enemy of rationality and goals, yet needs them as a means—then art centers itself on this irrational telos. Thus it deploys undiminished rationality in its procedures, even as, confined as it is by relations of production to the so-called technical world, it remains irrational at its core.

It may at first seem contradictory that Adorno stresses, on the one hand, the factor of public interest in the beautiful, a constitutive element of a materialist aesthetics, and, on the other, the Kantian motif of disinterestedness in the object felt to be beautiful, which is essential for Kant's understanding of the aesthetic dimension as such.

For Kant, "taste is the capacity to judge an object or an aesthetic presentation with pleasure or displeasure, without any personal interest. The object of such pleasure is called beautiful." As with the autonomy of the work of art, Adorno understands aesthetic disinterestedness as both real and merely apparent. He sees the essential impulse of *l'art pour l'art*, the aestheticism and art of the turn of the twentieth century, to be the uprising against the instrumental reason of bourgeois society, which tolerates nothing that opposes the principles of efficient, business-centered rationality. Thereby the original bourgeois and enlightened motif of social self-interest is, in Bloch's phrase, distorted into recognizability. If self-interest was once indispensable for human emancipation and for the ideological critique of illusions generated by clerical and feudal legitimations of domination, it has become, in the twentieth century, itself a component of the ideology of bourgeois society. Anything lacking in substantial interest for the processes of production and exchange that cannot be, in a word, exploited, falls out of contemporary man's system of coordinates for registering and evaluating things. Hence Adorno's anachronistic reference to this idea from Kant's prebourgeois aesthetics. In the work of Baudelaire, the poet of modern life, Stendhal's cryptomaterialist theory of beauty is specifically mentioned, while Kant's categorical rejection of the fixation on the use-value of beauty lives on without being mentioned, and only then achieves its full meaning. The spiritual physiognomy of the modern artist, which Baudelaire both described and embodied, is defined as much by the obliviousness of the subject who is capable of aesthetic experience, of rejecting self-interest and embracing the external world, as it is by that subject's attitude of rejection toward the bourgeois world of commodities.

According to Kant, "beauty is the shape of an object's purposefulness, to the extent that this is communicated without any image of purpose." The beautiful is not purposeless, but is what we can sense and experience without being dominated by the pressure to evaluate the object solely from the perspective of its purposefulness, in other words, the pressure to relate it to a category outside its own identity. Thus understood, beauty is not the abstract negation of the purposeful, but a suspension of the compulsory character of purposefulness.

It permits a free image of noncommodified purposefulness, inherent in the object itself, to enter the realm of experience. Such purposefulness, free of all compulsion, is possible because of humanity's capacity to emancipate itself from nature through purpose-oriented behavior. This purposefulness presupposes this capacity, but does not turn it into an absolute. Rather, it opens the utopian perspective of a freedom from the compulsory rationality of a means-ends framework; in such a world, people and things would no longer owe their right to exist to a functionality imposed from without, but could live as themselves. As Adorno puts it:

> Beauty is the exodus of what was objectified in the functional world—from that world. Kant's purposefulness without purpose is a principle that migrates from empirical reality, from the world of mandatory self-preservation, into a zone withdrawn from this, formerly a sacred world. Speaking dialectically, the purposefulness of works of art is a critique of the practical prescription of purposes. It takes a stand for the nature that has been repressed; in so doing it crystallizes the idea of a purposefulness other than that prescribed by humankind; the latter, to be sure, was effectively dissolved by natural science. Art is the salvation of nature or immediacy by means of their negation, perfect communication. It resembles a world free of control by means of unlimited control over its material; that is what is concealed in Kant's oxymoron.

The striving of self-conscious art for autonomy is, however, shaped by a tendency toward total independence, which for Adorno bears ideological features.

> In the nineteenth century, aesthetic appearance had intensified into fantasmagoria. Works of art covered up the traces of their moment of production.... This tendency was dominant until deep into modernity. The works' character as appearance strengthened itself into a claim on absoluteness ... Modernity then rebelled against the appearance of appearance, contending that it was no such thing.

The necessary fixation on the sphere of beautiful appearance brings the fetish character of artworks into being and, as a result, hardens autonomous art against the impulse driving the avant-garde of the twentieth century toward a suspension of aesthetic autonomy based on the division of labor. The new program is to move beyond aesthetic appearance to a successful life praxis of willingly social human beings. The conception of beauty without appearance acquires a social, liberating shape. Adorno writes, in the aphorism from *Minima Moralia* cited above, that as "true and beyond appearance, beauty could ultimately reveal itself as merely corporeal and real: in the very process of the end of art. Every work of art aims at such a culmination by willing the death of all other works."

Every work, it is here assumed, implicitly claims to represent in itself the entire genre. Works of art do not get along well; they cannot peacefully coexist in a museum's neutralizing atmosphere. Every work directs itself at the totality that is represented both in its formulation of issues and in its actual existence.

> That all art intends its own finality is another way of saying the same thing. Artworks' drive toward self-destruction, their deepest tendency, which is directed at the image of beauty without appearance—these repeatedly provoke the supposedly useless aesthetic disputes. Even as these disputes defiantly and stubbornly seek what is aesthetically right, in the very process falling victim to an insatiable dialectic, they achieve, against their will, a truer justice: through the power of the artworks that they organize and elevate into concepts, they limit the scope of each one individually, thus working toward the destruction of art—which is art's salvation.

The Silence of Music

Nowhere did Adorno formulate his aesthetic theory more penetratingly than in the field of music. His philosophy of music places the history and experiential content of music against the background of the bourgeois story of rationality and emancipation. In the context of Weber's sociological category of the "progressive rationalization of music," Adorno reads modern music as the rise and fall of subjective freedom, shaped aesthetically by the immanent logic of its forms.

Music history, as Max Weber has shown above all, is a story of progressive rationalization, that is, progressive control of nature's material. In the spirit of this tendency, music displays throughout an autonomous, self-enclosed realm.... If one looks at music history, or even the work of a single composer, to some extent from outside, then the story reveals, despite this autonomy, its social aspect. Its progressive rationalization appears as the sublimated expression of work processes, increasingly and systematically evident since the age of industrialization. The works of individual composers, however strictly focused on technical solutions, breathe the social air of their period.... The transitions from one style to the next are at the same time transitions of social structure.

Music's developing emancipation from the prescriptions of social function and of style, and from musical material's resistance to these prescriptions—in short, the composer's increasingly free relation to his material—is thus for Adorno always also an emancipation of second nature. Progressive autonomy of compositional method is progressive mastery over nature in the form of available material, which is subjected to the logic of harmonious organization and structure. The more that happens, the greater the potential for humanity in classical music and, in the music of free atonality, the potential for freedom, spontaneity, and subjective expression. Yet this increase in freedom is, for Adorno, inseparable from its opposite: the heteronomous identification of both material and the composer-subject through the pressures of compositional procedures that harden into a system, thus once again limiting the scope of subjective freedom that they once helped to enhance.

Through the governing category of "clarification"—which, unlike Arnold Gehlen, he views not as a thoroughly positive anthropological category but as inherently contradictory—Adorno reconstructs the developmental logic of modern compositional procedures as a dialectic of the subject's liberation and enslavement, to the point of its becoming virtually superfluous. As we saw in chapter 1, while working on the philosophy of new music during his Californian exile, Adorno helped Thomas Mann with his work on the novel *Doktor Faustus*; among other things, he transmitted the origins of the twelve-tone system directly to Mann's literary imagination and helped to formulate the conceptions of the composer Leverkühn's works. Adorno sees in the twelve-tone technique "the first great phenomenon of clarification in the new music" that was to help the listener, as Eduard Steuermann had put it, "to accomplish what the end itself could not manage at every moment." In *Doktor Faustus* this central idea is articulated in phrases that allude to Adorno's argument about the spoken quality of musical language and to his conception of musical material.[2]

> One would have to go on from here and make larger words out of the twelve letters, as it were, of the tempered semitone alphabet. Words of twelve letters, certain combinations and interrelations of the twelve semitones, series of notes *from* which a piece and all the movements of a work must strictly derive. Every note of the whole composition, both melody and harmony, would have to show its relation to this fixed fundamental series. Not one might recur until the other notes have sounded. Not one might appear which did not fulfill its function in the whole structure. There would no longer be a free note. . . . Rational organization through and through, one might indeed call it. . . . One must incorporate into the system all possible techniques of variation . . . that is, the means which once helped the "development" to win its hold over the sonata. I ask myself why I practiced so long . . . the devices of the old counterpoint and covered so much paper with inversion fugues, crabs, and inversions of crabs. Well now, all that should come in handy for the ingenious modification of the twelve-note word. In addition to being a fundamental series it could find application in this way, that every one of its intervals is replaced by its inversion. Again, one could begin the figure with its last note and finish it on its first, and then invert this figure as well. . . . four modes, each of which can be transposed to all the twelve notes of the chromatic scale, so that forty-eight different versions of the basic series may be used in a composition. . . . The way you describe the thing, it comes to a sort of composing before composition. The whole disposition and organization of the material would have to be ready when the actual work should begin, and all one asks is: which is the actual work? For this preparation of the material is done by variation, and the cre-

ative element in variation, which one might call the actual composition, would be transferred back to the material itself—together with the freedom of the composer. When he went to work, he would no longer be free.... Bound by a self-imposed compulsion to order, hence free. . . . Well, of course the dialectic of freedom is unfathomable. [*Doktor Faustus*, 191–93]

In the framework of the philosophy of music, this is the dialectic of freedom and constraint which, in Adorno's view, is not to be idealistically dissolved through the transfiguration of constraint into an aesthetically internalized, supposedly authentic freedom. For Adorno, music does not simply mirror the socially current relation between freedom and unfreedom; it does not translate social happenings into their aesthetic counterparts. But it must be involved in what Hegel calls historical substance. Adorno writes that "Beethoven did not adapt himself to the ideology of the often-cited rising bourgeoisie of the era around 1789 or 1800; rather, he embodied its spirit. Hence his unsurpassed success." The "double character of art [as] social fact and autonomous entity" maintains in authentic works a tension between internal formal principle and social experiential content. It is a central idea of Adorno's aesthetics that artworks can absorb social content only if they are overtly autonomous, that is, if they resist external functional constraints and obey only the moods and demands emanating from the formal shaping of the material. Here too Adorno connects dialectically to Kant, specifically to Kant's previously cited central thesis: "Beauty is the form of an object's purposefulness, to the extent this purposefulness is experienced without the concept of a purpose."

Adorno sees this as one side of the ambivalence of artworks: they may not be subject to a heteronomous, functional definition of purpose, but are accountable only to themselves; as formal structures they are nevertheless purposefully organized. This is how artworks retain social and historical elements in mediated form; that is why they require an interpretation informed by social theory and the philosophy of history. Their "transition" from freedom into the system of aesthetically self-generated, compulsory order is, for Adorno, ambivalent, both a break and a dialectical transition. This transition "occurred early in the heroic period of free atonality." This "musical freedom style" was in his view defined by the attempt to realize "the idea of unchecked freedom without concessions." In contrast, the "transition from the experiences of free atonality to the systemic formulation of twelve-tone technique" also involved a moment of the heteronomous creation of order. The system did not emerge primarily from the needs articulated in the musical material itself—not, that is, "from the inherent truth of the object"—but from the subject's need for firm structures. Yet, on the other hand, the strict logic of the twelve-tone technique, which subordinates the organization of musical time and musical narrative to a logical principle, also arose consistently from music's need to define itself, a need that ultimately underlies the freedom that was the goal of atonality. In the course of further developments, Adorno contended, autonomy was deployed as an argument against serialism itself. For more recent composers such as Pierre Boulez and Karlheinz Stockhausen, it had become clear that the full logic of autonomy had by no means been developed in serialism. At this point the dialectic between freedom and determinism, to which the new music is subject, becomes clear. "The school that emerged from serialism sought to radicalize the twelve-tone principle, to extend it to all musical dimensions, to elevate it into a totality. Absolutely everything was to be predetermined, including the dimensions that are still free in Schoenberg: rhythm, meter, tone color, and overall structure." All musical parameters are reduced to the "common denominator of time. . . . But this process makes one uneasy. The commodification already noticeable in twelve-tone technique, namely, the inhibition of the living, auditory performance as music's essential constituent, is intensified into a threat to destroy any and all meaningful context."

Meaning is not an absolute category for Adorno: "The story of modern art is to a great extent the story of metaphysical loss of meaning, unfolding with irrefutable logic." That goes against the pretension that meaning defines the norm of an art, music, that in modernity has included meanings necessary destruction as part of its own structural law. But the abstract negation of coherent goals, the perspective of which, no matter how disguised, is ultimately that of a meaningful, humane, just life, would be the wrong outcome.

[Even art's] loss of meaning, which it adopts as if willing its own destruction, or seeking to maintain its life through an antidote, cannot remain its final word, its intentions notwithstanding. The nonknowledge of the emphatically absurd work of art, in the style of Beckett, marks a point of indifference between meaning and its negation; and anyone who might read, with relief, positive meaning into this indifference would be offending against it. At the same time, one can not conceive of a work of art that, even as it integrates everything alien into itself and rejects its own context of meaning, does not create new meaning regardless. Metaphysical and aesthetic meaning are not indivisible, not even today.

Adorno does not see the "threat to destroy any meaning-based context" as a blow for freedom against the false claims of holistic, integrated meaning—which for him would be wholly appropriate. Rather, the threat means that, not only for the structurally involved listener but also for the composing subject, absolute relief from metaphysics in the form of total freedom over material turns into unfreedom, causing music itself to lose its substance.[3] The apparent help for the composer "puts him on the spot. He is subordinated to a version of law that is strange to him and which he can hardly grasp. The resulting music turns into something deaf and empty."

In the 1950s Adorno, as course director and participant in Darmstadt and Kranichstein, the centers of new music in Germany, both followed and influenced the musical developments of his era. It was therefore through strong personal empathy, not through an aesthetic concretization of Hegel's historical dialectic, that he was able to decode the so-called aleatory style embodied in the music of John Cage and Maurizio Kagel as the necessary antithesis to this tendency toward "closure." Adorno writes that the principle of musical chance

> sought to break out of the total determinism, the integral, obligatory musical ideal of the serial school . . . but in fact the principle of chance launched by Cage remained as alien to the subject as its seeming opposite, the serial principle; it too belongs to the category of relief for the enfeebled self. To be sure, pure chance disrupts the tedium of necessity without exit—but it is no less distant from the experience of the living ear.

Certainly Cage was right to sensitize us to what is false "about the blind ideal of total musical control over nature," but his own work did not truly transcend "the style of nature control." Adorno points out that György Ligeti, on the basis of his own experience as a composer, took note of the aesthetic and historical-philosophical dialectic of freedom which was also the focus of Thomas Mann and Adorno in *Doktor Faustus*. Ligeti "drew attention to the fact that, in their impact, the extremes of absolute determinism and absolute chance coincide."

It appears that Ligeti's compositions were, for Adorno, thoroughly equal to the task of addressing this point. Adorno himself offers no exit from the dialectical tangle embodied in the new music, neither on a practical level nor on a theoretical level. At the beginning of the 1960s he argued emphatically, and with a new avant-garde momentum, for a "musique informelle" that would be a necessary contemporary figure for the musical style of freedom. But he did not depict its shape positively, and certainly did not conceive it as a blessed rebirth of earlier authentic forms:

> the most serious difficulty, however, is that despite everything, there is no going back. If, in the face of twelve-tone technique, serialism, and the aleatory style, one endeavored simply to reactivate subjective freedom, that is to say, free atonality as expressed in Schoenberg's *Erwartung* (1909), one would inevitably become a virtual reactionary.

In all his writings on the art of the twentieth century, Adorno is invariably concerned with "recognizing the objective antinomies in which art that is true to its own inherent claims, without obsessing about outcomes, is inevitably entangled within a heteronomous reality." These antinomies "cannot be overcome . . . except by carrying on their conflict, without illusions, to its end." The epistemological endurance of the antinomies defines the shape of Adorno's dialectical aesthetics of modernity. But this road to a potential exit contains the possibility of music's falling silent, and of the false image of the end of art. Adorno must remain undecided on this point. As a dialectician he discerns, in the threat of the false end of art, the spark of art's true transformation. For him it could only be music that would still now be possible by "measuring itself against its extreme negation, its own silence." The refusal of "meaning" or "statement" that marked the advanced art of the 1950s and 1960s is, for Adorno, by no means nihilistic resignation or helplessness. It is instead a logical shaping of aesthetic material in close accord with the objective historical condition of the world in which art is embedded. Awareness of its negativity is generated precisely by art that seems to withdraw entirely from this reality:

> Consistent negation of aesthetic meaning would be possible only through the abolition of art. The most recent important artworks articulate the nightmare of such abolition, while at the same time, through their very existence, struggling against being abolished; as if the end of art threatened the end of a humanity whose very suffering mandates art, an art that does not soothe and understate suffering. This art dreams for humanity its destruction, precisely so that it should wake up, stay in control, survive.

The Transition from Art to Knowledge

The central ideas of Adorno's aesthetics, as presented here, show that he did not, as it is often assumed, resignedly withdraw from the objective aporias of critical philosophy and social theory into the supposedly peaceful realm of aesthetics. One can already see that, even as a young man, he refused to choose between music and philosophy. But even apart from that, Adorno's view of artworks themselves makes clear that he was always working on a theory of aesthetics. Related to the motif of a philosophy in the perspective of redemption was a discussion of the correspondences and similarities between negatively dialectical philosophy and art. These relations occur in the zone focused on the experience of what Adorno, using an expression from Edmund Husserl's phenomenology, terms "things in themselves." For Adorno, it is the mission of both critical philosophy and authentic art to translate, without distortion, the being of things into media so that we are able to recognize and experience it. Adorno shares with Hegel the assumption that the goal of art is knowledge. This assumption is an element of the discourse about the end of art as art. For Adorno, the end of art is the dimension specific to modern art. Art itself begins to reflect on its double relation to its objects and to its own formal laws.

Adorno's views can be clarified by literature, specifically by studying the construction of Marcel Proust's *In Search of Lost Time*. The work contains meditations, similar to Henri Bergson's philosophy, about experience and the concept of time, and on the author's relation to his story and its articulation in the novel.[4] *Doktor Faustus*, too, is paradigmatic for the transition from art to knowledge: the work is defined essentially by the constant border crossing between fictional narration and conceptually conceived aesthetics. On the other side knowledge is in quest of possibilities that it does not have in its categorical repertoire. Philosophy is increasingly conscious of the artificiality of its conceptual structures. That self-consciousness brings it closer to art. Yet for Adorno the point is not to blur the distinctions between philosophy and art, but rather to probe the territory in which each enterprise is designed to refer to the other. Philosophy needs art in order to reach "things in themselves"; art needs philosophy, above all, in order to decode through concepts its concept-free form of knowledge. As Adorno writes in *Aesthetic Theory*, "Aesthetics presents philosophy with the bill for having been degraded by academe into a separate field."

> [Aesthetics] demands from philosophy precisely what philosophy neglects: that it should extract phenomena from their mere existence and contain them in self-contemplation, as reflections of what has become frozen within knowledge systems, not as autonomous elements of their own system. Thereby aesthetics bows before what its object, like any other, desires immediately and directly. In order to be fully experienced, every artwork needs thought—and that means philosophy, which is nothing but thought that refuses to be curbed.... Art emphatically *is* knowledge, but not knowledge of objects. An artwork is understood only when it is grasped as a complex expression of truth. This complexity inescapably affects its relation to untruth, both inside and outside itself; any other judgment of artworks remains incidental.

Ideally, art and philosophy could partially release each other from the pressures placed on them by the relation between nature and spirit, distorted by its formation through domination. But this can happen only in occasional fortunate moments; for now, the essential task of art and philosophy is, Adorno writes, to "render suffering eloquent," not to anticipate the better world through a "preview."

As Kurt Lenk writes,

> the cognitive function that Adorno ascribes to authentic art . . . is based on its capacity to generate experiences not yet regulated by the system of the administered world and to give them a language. Art's task, as it were, is to rescue once again what is totally lacking in the standardizing, conceptually fixed social thinking that endlessly reproduces things as they are. Art thereby becomes a kind of counterpoint to the all-dominating culture industry, which ceaselessly eternalizes the existing social condition only by replicating it. While the ideological control of the masses structures their mentalities once again for the ruling classes' purposes, rendering void any potential thought of possible alternatives that might occur to them, art, at the point where it invokes accurate fantasies, still generates utopian images of a better world.

As Adorno sees it, the social tendency toward a false abolition of art continues. The aesthetic difference from things as they are is constantly reduced. In jazz, which Adorno views as the culture industry's quintessential musical form, two elements define the process: the feigned rhythmic interruption of the musical process (which in fact continues, structured by the "dogged unit of the basic pulse") and the "standardization" and "pseudo-individualizing" that he sees as its defining musical characteristics. Hence, Adorno declares, "Jazz is the false liquidation of art; instead of utopia being actualized, it disappears from the picture." Adorno is not being entirely fair to jazz. He tries to interpret its basic aesthetic shape psychoanalytically, as the voluntary submission of the musical subject to the ever-present social threat of castration. This interpretation may still be enlightening when considering musical clichés such as those of Paul Whiteman, whose dance orchestra the young Adorno probably heard in Frankfurt—if one shares the socio-cultural view that the gestures of entertainment music prevalent in the transition from a liberal to an authoritarian society have something in common with the growing pressure to conform in an emerging mass society. But this interpretation was no longer true for the harmonic and rhythmic subtleties of swing music by Benny Goodman, Teddy Wilson, and Lionel Hampton. In the 1930s Adorno was convinced that radio listeners who enjoy hearing Ella Fitzgerald sing "A Tisket, A Tasket" accompanied by Chick Webb's orchestra must be sadomasochistic individuals in Erich Fromm's sense, stomping on their secret longing for the return of childhood happiness. Adorno fails to understand performative, ironizing styles in popular music; he is able to hear them only idiosyncratically and to stylize them promptly as images of those social tendencies that he (with good reason) rejects. On the other hand, Adorno publicly justifies, in 1933, the Nazis' prohibition against jazz. His dangerous, quasi-Hegelian argument asserts that jazz is untrue as an art form, in any case finished: "there's nothing here to rescue." Jazz is not "art music" but "bad musical craft": "the consumer music of the upper middle classes in the postwar years." The art of differentiation that normally characterizes Adorno's aesthetic analyses, the proximity to the material and its structuring in his close readings—all this disappears from his writings on jazz. The German jazz guitarist Volker Kriegel, who in the 1960s studied sociology with Adorno, reported that Adorno was clearly unfamiliar with the names Charlie Parker and John Coltrane, let alone their music. However, although Adorno's critique of jazz is erroneous in strictly musical terms, it remains of systemic interest, as, in his dialectical theory of culture and his critique of the culture industry, the idea of the defined negation of things as they are is further developed.

Theorizing Art and Culture in the Institute for Social Research

Critical theory was understood by its proponents as the conceptual articulation of structural and historical landmarks of high- and late-capitalist society, and of its antagonisms. This articulation was both materialist and normative; it was enabled by concepts that describe what is and anticipate both what is to be expected and also what is possible. From the outset, both art and aesthetic theories had a high standing in the research program of critical theory. The first volume of the *Journal of Social Research* (1932) included the programmatic essays "On the Social Position of Literature" by Leo Löwenthal and "On the Social Position of Music" by Adorno. These essays do not propose, as their titles and the condition of the sociology of art at that time might suggest, sociological reductions of aesthetic contents to the social position of their producers. Rather, they offer exemplary portrayals of how social experiences are expressed in aesthetic objects, which, while never self-sufficient, may well be autonomous as artworks.

Löwenthal deems it the task of literary studies, inspired by sociology, history, economics, and social psychology, "to investigate which specific social structures find expression in the individual literary work, and what function the individual work exercises in society. . . . Questions of form, both that of motif and that of subject matter, must be opened in the same way to the materialist perspective." Comparable formal methods such as open dialogues or authorial restriction on commentary are made transparent via the differing meanings they convey at different social and historical stages. For example, Löwenthal compares the work of the Young German Karl Gutzkow with the impressionism of Theodor Fontane and Arthur Schnitzler. He shows that "the modern conversation about bourgeois society" in Gutzkow's work brings to the surface the post-traditional conception of informed, autonomous subjects in a liberal context open to new outcomes—and with it the confidence about individual possibilities. By contrast, the explicit withdrawal in works of Fontane and Schnitzler was driven by insecurity. This insecurity resulted, on the one hand, in the inability to conceive coherent new theories underpinning the authors' own literary production; on the other, it substantiated the self-critical sensibility of the liberal bourgeoisie, who sensed that time was running out on their era.

Löwenthal's method is based in the theory of reflection, but it is free of the problematic omission of autonomous aesthetic logic, which, under Communist orthodoxy, rapidly turned this method into a schematic instrument for testing and monitoring fundamental beliefs. Interpreting a literary work's aesthetic meaning and decoding its social perspective are, for Löwenthal, inseparable.

The Frankfurt School authors viewed the turn toward acknowledging a genuine formal logic in artworks as a development of great importance for immanent aesthetic analysis, and therefore as an expression of social conditions in itself. Adorno's famous formula, which alludes to Durkheim, in his *Aesthetic Theory*—the claim that an artwork is always both autonomous and socially conditioned—is the aesthetic-sociological compass for the contributions to the *Journal for Social Research* written by himself, Löwenthal, Herbert Marcuse, Horkheimer, and Benjamin. It is also true for Kracauer, who like Benjamin occupied a marginal position in the institution but nonetheless played an important role in the development of Frankfurt School theory.

This formula of the artwork as both autonomous and socially conditioned has implications for aesthetics, sociology of art, and philosophy of history. These implications are as follows: artworks articulate both subjective and objective historical-social experiences and understandings, and they do so in a specific way, not conceptual but living; thus these historical articulations are always also manifestations of aesthetic freedom. Art's autonomy, its "achievement of independence from society," is for Adorno a "function of the bourgeois sense of freedom."

From this perspective, we can perceive the social dialectic of art's production and reception: freedom is the consistent resistance to functionalism, the imperative of an increasingly self-conscious aesthetics, yet it emerges functionally from a social need. But this double perspective is always also philosophical. While the intellectual contents of artworks become accessible to the audience and interpreters through their material dimension, their truth contents can be conceptualized only by analyzing their formal rules (and the relation of these rules to the material dimension). If aesthetic claims of validity are not to be merely relativized by the elucidation of their social origins, a philosophical theory of aesthetics is indispensable.

Artworks, Marcuse contends, render audible or visible what is and what could be, by shaping their contents tangibly and semantically, by organizing them through laws of structure. Art is a form of knowledge, a language that is sui generis, at once communication and expression. This knowledge is structured by the style of individual constructs, through the formal principle according to which their components are crystallized into an organized relation to the work as a whole. Through this process, Marcuse explained years later in 1968, art arrives at an oppositional stance toward everyday praxis, even as it shares the human concerns of the everyday: "By creating its own form, its own 'language', art moves in a dimension of reality that confronts the everyday world antagonistically—but in such a way that words, sounds, music, in their transforming, indeed transfiguring, of their initiating everyday images, 'preserve' these images' forgotten or distorted truth by endowing them with their own 'beautiful' shape, harmony, dissonance, rhythm, etc." From the first essays in the *Journal for Social Research* to the final works of Adorno and Marcuse, the aesthetics of critical theory was always a historical philosophical aesthetics. The core assumption of the critical theorists was that in modernity the emancipation of works of art is correlated with the emancipation of the human subject. Both processes of emancipation, the thesis holds, are riven by the same inner contradiction, that of progress in bourgeois society. The increasing autonomy of artworks anticipates that of the subject, and the same is true with respect to their failure. Thus, for critical theory, aesthetic emancipation is not a *reflection* of social emancipation, but its *model*. According to this perspective, art bears the same relation to mass culture that a radical utopian vision bears to shallow vicarious satisfaction. To put the claim schematically: truth and ideology interact both in the autonomous art of bourgeois society and in mass culture. For Adorno and Horkheimer, mass culture defines the late form of bourgeois society.

Adorno advanced this thesis in his essay "On the Fetish Character in Music and the Regression of Listening," published in the *Journal of Social Research* in 1938. In this text, he develops the paradigm for his critique of the culture industry. Art, he contends, maintains a promise of happiness, even when it is no longer "beautiful" but is radical modern art. In the aesthetic mirror appears "the image of a social condition," in which "the particular moments of happiness"—namely, the moments of unregimented experience of sensuous musical pleasure and authentic subjective expression—"would be more than simply appearance." The new music, Adorno claims, makes an ascetic break with appearance's promise of happiness, not in order to withhold happiness from its audience, but because it is drenched in the consciousness of aesthetic appearance's untruth. Already in the rituals of nineteenth-century bourgeois musical life, and then totally in the industrially produced and distributed mass culture of the early twentieth century, aesthetic appearance merely tantalized individual subjects by stimulating their senses and making available unlimited expressivity. Wherever pleasure, which is mediated by custom and sensuous experience, is misused by being functionalized for advertising purposes—in the sphere of art as well as in mass culture—then authentic art becomes forbidding, refusing functionalization but in the process losing its accessibility.

The social antagonism of a commodity-based society thus has consequences for the logic of aesthetics. Adorno's method consists in deducing the contradictions of cultural forms from the irreconcilable oppositions of social reality. The contradiction of authentic modern art lies in the fact that it is "objectively" an anticipation of non-mutilated experience and sensuous happiness. But in the present, where the aesthetic sphere is put wholly at the service of the logic of commodification, art can play its anticipatory role only negatively, by sealing itself off from communication and sensuous fulfillment. For Adorno, the contradiction of art for the masses, by contrast, lies in the fact that both its distribution system and its products suggest they will provide consumers with pleasure, freedom, and cultural self-determination; in fact, they merely extend heteronomous production and distribution of goods from the workday into the workers' free time. The aesthetically reactionary style of music hits, films, and bestsellers freezes their recipients at reactionary levels of response and awareness. That is the social function of the culture industry. Adorno and Horkheimer introduced this concept in *Dialectic of Enlightenment* to make clear that mass culture is no spontaneous, self-defined expression of the masses, but a structure designed by the ruling classes, serving the purposes of manipulation. The culture industry generates regressive needs, above all an infantile compulsion to repetition, which the industry then aims to satisfy with its always identical products. Consumers sense, more or less clearly, that the pleasures offered by the culture industry do not actually produce pleasure, but rather cause boredom. Adorno argues, however, alluding to Erich Fromm's analyses of character responsive only to authority, that consumers identify with the inevitable. Whereas autonomous artworks always open a window onto a utopia of liberation from the fixation on profit-driven, goal-oriented rationality, this perspective on the cultural other is barred in the mass art products of the culture industry. These products are ruled by the *totalized* transfer of economic criteria to cultural production, a transfer that is openly acknowledged. The use value of cultural goods is replaced by their exchange value. More precisely, it is not the cultural good itself that is enjoyed, but its exchange value. This is the case both in the world of entertainment and in the world of art, which is thought to be elevated and serious. Instead of extremes of oblivious pleasure tending toward the anarchic, or spontaneous identification with a musical or literary action (here Adorno means cognitive-structural identification), everywhere there prevails a fixation on just being there: which films one has seen, which bands and star conductors one has heard, or which books are essential to have read. The concertgoer's elevated feelings consist in demonstrating his social status and imagining that he contributes to the bourgeois practice of art by buying concert tickets. For Adorno, this bourgeois practice of art now exists only in ruins. He therefore counts it very much to the Marx Brothers' credit that they produced a film allegorizing the destruction of the genre of opera (*Animal Crackers*).

In advanced bourgeois society, Adorno argues, the concept of culture has always represented a sphere in which the laws of the practical world are at least partially suspended. By the terms "practical" and "praxis" Adorno means the realm of both the production and circulation of goods and the framing conditions of social domination and mastery of nature. Since capitalist market society, in the era of Henry Ford, turned into a series of authoritarian and monopolistic states, the advanced industrial mode of production has become a model for cultural reproduction. The subdividing of production into segments resulted in the dismantling of cultural awareness. "The montage character of the culture industry, the synthetic, controlled mode of production of its cultural objects" resulted in total social integration through the imposition of a media structure on all realms of life and experience. The result was the "false identity of general and particular." Cultural products became indistinguishable from one other because, unlike artworks, they no longer obeyed a logic specific to each work. Work and free time became ever more similar. As a universal, media-based process of amusement, the culture industry turned into the opposite of amusement, an extension of work into free time. The culture industry's function was to reproduce the existing world. Adorno declares, in his 1938 essay, that identification with social and economic rule was the core of the conformism of mass culture audiences. All pleasure was exclusively masochistic. The culture industry's objects were thoroughly commodified cultural goods. In the realm of music they were masked outwardly by familiarity and commercial success, inwardly by easily memorized moments such as distinctive melodies or catchy texts, by simple structures such as intensifying and repeating syncopations, and by isolated sense stimulations that remain particular and lacking any meaningful compositional relation to the totality of the musical structure, such as beautiful voices or the supposedly "exclusive" sound of unusual instruments and voluptuous orchestrations.

Before the time of emigration, Horkheimer's institute had sought to introduce to Germany the statistical methods of empirical social research in order to be able to answer key questions: how a society in objectively urgent need of revolution can obstinately resist the practical process of revolution, and why human beings seem to prefer aligning themselves with the authoritarian state instead of fighting for political and social freedom. In the United States, too, empirical methods of cultural sociology, which centered on the transmission of impacts and the recipients' habits of listening, viewing, and reading, seemed to Adorno inadequate to the task of gaining a structural understanding of mass culture. He decided against a purely neutral description, and later evaluation, of the phenomena engaging him in his collaboration on the Princeton Radio Research Project. Instead, he tried to deduce the basis of the audience's reactions in social antagonisms and their aesthetic correlates. Critical theory of culture and aesthetics is for him a philosophical theory, meaning that modes of consumption are to be derived from relations of production, which themselves are not to be understood as ultimate givens, but to be traced back to the dialectical concept of society as a whole. This methodological perspective begins with the thesis that the audiences for contemporary mass culture, that is, most people in modern Western industrialized societies, are largely alienated from themselves, from their own products and modes of experience, and are cut off from the possibility of free self-determination. To the partly imposed, partly freely conforming "abandonment of individuality" belongs, as a kind of reward for going along, "the endowment of exchange value with affect."

Adorno's analyses are thus constructed in a strict categorical way, but he hardly, or no longer, tested them empirically. The result is the Nietzschean "pathos of distance" they maintain toward the fields they explore, for example toward radio listeners, who were discussed above in relation to Ella Fitzgerald. But classical music listeners fare no better. As Rolf Wiggershaus has written, "For Adorno, the way many people whistle a familiar tune in distorted form was the same as when children pull a dog's tail. The just as obvious alternative possibility, that it involved a variation on something familiar, a non-reverential adaptation of the well known—that he didn't consider worthy of mention." This blind spot differentiates Adorno's perspective from that of cultural studies, which is especially interested in deviant and heterodox appropriations of cultural material by its users. But even though Adorno's results often lack convincing empirical data, they are frequently on the mark aesthetically: for example, his observation that in mass culture, as a rule, what is experienced as close and intimate is actually most alien from individual experience, namely, the standard output of the "mainstream"—whereas avant-garde art, which "endeavors to speak for the speechless," is felt to be profoundly alien and is therefore rejected by most people. Adorno insinuates that people far from the avant-garde essentially have only the false choice of remaining silent or breaking into a fascist howl; this made him deaf to the aesthetically and socially productive sides of mass culture.

Benjamin and Kracauer: Theorizing Mass Art

Whereas Adorno begins his philosophical analysis of mass art and culture with the assumption that they are antithetical to autonomous art, Benjamin proposes ideas aiming to transform the very concept of art. For Benjamin, new industrial technologies generate new aesthetic techniques of representation and expression, which in turn produce new modalities of perception and articulation. In his famous essay "The Work of Art in the Age of Mechanical Reproduction," Benjamin presents a new theory of the aesthetic that abandons the distinction between high and low art. In the process, he sketches the outline of a utopia of mass art. His starting points are the aesthetic views of two very different authors: Paul Valéry's modernist aesthetic of autonomous art and Bertolt Brecht's political, reality-based poetics and media theory.

Valéry provides intrinsic aesthetic reflections on the substantial changes to which the twentieth-century artwork is exposed. Valéry was the first to point out how modern science and social practices affect art and alter its internal and external structure. Technical innovations change both the arts themselves and the theoretical concept of art. He recognized that modern technology tends toward reproduction, both in art and in the realm of sensory awareness in general, and he anticipated the modern technology of entertainment, which would deliver images and sounds into people's homes, just like water, gas, and electricity.

From Brecht, Benjamin borrows the insistence on developing a new aesthetic approach that would be "completely unusable" for fascist purposes, specifically for the fascist "aestheticization of politics." At that time, it was clear that both Italian fascism and German Nazism had outwardly ambivalent but unmistakably goal-oriented attitudes toward technical innovations. Radical modernization is the reverse side of the attempts to reanimate dead traditions and the artificial creation of cultural pseudo-archaisms. In Italy the fascist aesthetic, inspired by Futurism, was thoroughly involved with the twentieth-century avant-garde; it blatantly exploited radical modernism, but not without an inward, material affinity for it. In Germany, by contrast, following in the wake of the internationally well-regarded author Ernst Jünger, synthetic art movements such as "heroic realism" were dreamed up, and political events were staged, as aesthetic events via the newest technology, for their impact on the masses. The authoritarian mass society is shaped with the help of the latest advances in the mass media.

Benjamin recognizes such political staging as the vicarious satisfaction of the new need of working people for political and cultural self-determination. Instead of enabling the masses to achieve their "right," namely, a revolutionizing of property relations, the National Socialists endowed them with "expression"—one that is not authentically their own. Together with Brecht, Benjamin advances thoughts on how radio could be made useful for progressive social revolutions. With this starting point he develops a materialist theory of modern media, together with their social premises and consequences.

Benjamin's new categories, which are "useless to rightists," are the criteria of "cult value" and "exhibition value" with which he distinguishes between archaic, religiously oriented, feudal, and bourgeois practices deploying art. Although in its beginnings art had been part of the rituals of magic and religion, in bourgeois society the work of art became valued for its uniqueness. Cult value, deriving its legitimacy from an assumed involvement with the sacred, is replaced by exhibition value. Verified genuineness and the work's spatiotemporal presence in a given place came to define the aesthetic experience and the evaluation of artistic production. However, as soon as artworks are no longer distinguished by their uniqueness and individual authenticity, the criterion of exhibition value loses its meaning. Technology now becomes the core concept.

For Benjamin, photography and film are the genuinely modern artistic genres. They are defined by the fact that technical reproducibility is not something secondary to them, as with music and the visual arts, but constitutes an essential element of their structure, perhaps the most essential. The nineteenth-century debate about whether photography was an art in the same way painting was turned out to be a phantom debate, because the decisive question had not been posed: "whether the invention of photography had not transformed the whole nature of art." But that is precisely what happened; photography, and soon thereafter film, conquered "their own special place among artistic procedures." In film, internal technique—the formal law of the artwork—and external technique, the technology of production and that of distribution, became one.

Benjamin views his aesthetics of film as "unusable" for National Socialism because film, through its new relation to technology, shatters and liquidates tradition. Its revolutionizing of art contributed substantially, at the level of both aesthetics and theory of perception, to the social revolution. "The technology of reproduction detaches the reproduced item from the realm of tradition. By multiplying reproduction, this technology replaces the work's unique occurrence with vast numbers of its manifestations. And by permitting the reproductive process to engage the audience in all possible situations, the technology makes actual the work being reproduced. These two processes lead to a violent rupture of what has been handed down—a rupture of humanity. These processes are closely tied to the mass movement of our days. Their most powerful agent is film. Its social importance is . . . unthinkable without its destructive, cathartic side: the liquidation of the value of tradition in cultural heritage." In the reception of autonomous artworks, the decisive element was the experience of their uniqueness, of their individual distinctiveness and spatiotemporal specificity, which Benjamin describes with the metaphor (borrowed from Ludwig Klages) of the "auratic." But what now characterizes the reception of artworks at the highest level is the disintegration of the aura. Films and the transparent architecture of the Bauhaus "have no aura." For Benjamin, art in the age of technological reproduction is mass art. Huge numbers of works are produced, with the masses as their intended audience. Mass culture, an outcome of "the increasing importance of the masses in everyday life," is, Benjamin argues, defined by a "passionate interest of today's masses": the need to "make things spatially and humanly more accessible."

In the 1920s, Siegfried Kracauer based his theory of cinema on the thought that urban transformations in the capitalist industrial societies of the twentieth century generate a need for a specific culture that is both affluent and legitimate. In his late, realistic film theory he then juxtaposes the concept of autonomous art with its antithesis, non-autonomous art, which has a quite different relation to the external reality that artists engage: Kracauer ascribes to the cinematic medium the materialist power to "rescue external reality." In contrast, Benjamin alters the concept of autonomy. Normally, the phrase "autonomy of art" implies the process of art's emancipation from the functional context in which it is harnessed, framed by ritual, religion, social cult, and the representation of power. In modernity—according to the theorizing of autonomy in relation to Weber's theory of rationalization—art is liberated from the compulsion to serve heteronomous purposes. Benjamin turns the tables on this theory. He believes that ritual "cult value" *and* bourgeois "exhibition value" give art the fetishistic appearance of autonomy. In the art business of bourgeois society (not only in the art worship of the nineteenth century, though that is an obvious example) the cult status persisted, to which artworks owed both their origin and their appearance of being worthy of veneration. Only when "the age of its technical reproducibility separated art from its cult-based foundations did the appearance of its autonomy dissolve irrevocably."

As we saw in chapter 6, Benjamin, at this phase of his thinking, labels his solidarity with "bad new things" against "good old things" as a positive "new barbarism." The destruction of aura and autonomy, in his view, was the precondition of the enlightened grounding of art in politics. He regards this not just as a temporal strategy but as a superior insight into the phenomenon of art. Since art is always defined by its social functions and reception contexts, Benjamin sees the idea of autonomy as ideology. In its "age of technical reproducibility," therefore, "the entire social function of art" is altered. "In place of its basis in ritual, art becomes based in a different practice: its basis in politics." Art becomes a political phenomenon because the masses appropriate it through technologies and perceptual habits. New modes of reception correspond to the new technologies and the collective sensory capacity changes with the new media, as is apparent in phenomena such as "accelerated perception" or "the optical unconscious." Benjamin decodes experiences of modern urban life—the atomization of processes of living, sensory consciousness, and reflection—as levels of articulation of the formal language imposed by the new medium, film. In addition to the techniques of cutting and montage, which turned images into projectiles striking people, Benjamin focuses on cinema as a new mode of collective, simultaneous reception. Art becomes a mass phenomenon in a double sense: artworks become accessible to the masses and the masses appear as an active subject, receiving and producing art. Benjamin borrows this concept too from Kracauer. Contemporary artworks, he contends, no longer demand contemplation; they respond to the needs of working people, who encounter art in a state of "distraction."

Adorno's thinking is bound dialectically to the aesthetics of the autonomous artwork, which he reads as a totality either fulfilling or refusing meaning; the elements of this totality owe their existential justification to the overall coherent context created by the artistic subject. Like Benjamin, Kracauer takes a different path. In his 1960 book *Theory of Film* he writes, "However realistic the [traditional] artist may be, he overpowers reality rather than recording it. And since he is free to pursue his own formal inclinations, his work can be shaped into a meaningful whole. Hence the meaning of the aesthetic whole defines the meaning of its elements; or, conversely, its elements have meaning only insofar as they contribute to the truth or beauty inherent in the work as a whole. Its function is not to reflect reality but to actualize a vision of it." In contrast to Adorno, it is not axiomatic for Kracauer that the aesthetic, in its ever more self-conscious attitude toward objectivity, is necessarily destined either to become increasingly absorbed in itself—that is, in the autonomy of art—or to fail catastrophically (or both). On this point, Kracauer's theory differs fundamentally from Adorno's apocalyptic aesthetics. This is not just because his theory is not essentially framed by the history of philosophy; it is also focused much more strongly on the visual realm, with its specifically visual modes of awareness, than on the constructive realm of notated musical forms. Over time, Kracauer developed his early ideologically critical film theory of the 1920s into a variant of aesthetic realism, influenced by Erwin Panofsky's visual theory and constituting an alternative to the aesthetic realism of Lukács. For Kracauer, film is the aesthetic genre that can "rescue" external reality.

What does that mean? Kracauer contrasts the film as artwork with the autonomous artwork that "destroys" reality. The dialectical point in Kracauer's theory is that film is indeed antithetical to the autonomous artwork, but retains in common with it the attitude of opposing the utilitarian thinking of rationalized bourgeois society. This is Kracauer's primary concern when he argues for the rescue of apparent, physical, external reality.

"The material of film is external reality as such": this is the argument of Panofsky, who laid the theoretical foundation for acknowledging the film medium as an aesthetic genre. Kracauer followed him in this project. Film, Kracauer contended, works with "life in the raw." In other words, it can "reproduce reality, that is, our visible world." This reproduction of reality is not just a poor visual imitation of the world that delights the public; rather, it is only in film reproduction that reality becomes visible for us. Cinematic images are signs that have a specific, nonarbitrary relation to the denoted object. Films, at the height of their characteristic aesthetic potential, had the objective intention of "rescuing" the world's phenomena. These phenomena are to be saved from indifference and functional reduction, that is, from mutilation by the wear and tear to which a commodifying society exposes them. They are to be saved, too, from the reduction of meaning inflicted on them by the constricted perception of instrumentalized reason. But physical, manifest reality also needs rescuing from the degradation into amorphous matter inflicted by artists who can see in it only the material to be shaped into a meaningful aesthetic totality.

Aesthetically successful films capture images as raw material that "tells its own story"; they really show "what they show." Filmmakers are people who "dare to penetrate ever more deeply into the jungle of material phenomena, at the risk of losing themselves in it irrevocably." That is the ontological realism of Kracauer's film theory.

Anarchistic and Bourgeois Romanticism:
Adorno's Critique of Benjamin

Adorno derives the criteria for autonomous art from the aesthetics of music. The work's formal law is constituted by the coherent relation of the parts to the whole. That does not mean the logic of the whole dominates the parts, but that it gives a shape to the unfolding aesthetic experience that is revealed only in the experience of the parts, indeed through processing their structure and development. "Responsible art follows criteria that come close to cognition: consistent and inconsistent, true and false," Adorno writes. In his critique of Benjamin's concept of mass culture, Adorno designates autonomous artworks, which are responsible only to the truth content of their formal law, on the one hand, and functionally dependent products of consumer art on the other as the two violently separated "halves of aesthetic freedom": "Both bear the stigmata of capitalism, both contain elements of change. . . . The two are the torn-apart halves of aesthetic freedom, which, however, cannot be reconstituted by adding them together." Adorno would have called the unification of "high and low culture," in a society liberated from the antagonism between owners and workers, a false reconciliation. He is still convinced that "in a Communist society work is organized in such a way that people will no longer be so exhausted and dumbed down as to need distraction." But the claim that one must decide here and now between autonomous and "dependent" art is false: "to sacrifice the one to the other would be romantic, either in the bourgeois sense of conserving personality and all the associated magic, or in the anarchistic sense of trusting blindly in the historical self-empowerment of the proletariat: a proletariat which is itself produced in a bourgeois framework." Adorno's use of the concepts "romantic" and "anarchistic" is idiosyncratic but not inexact, in terms of the history of ideas. Romantic aesthetics was linked to the theory of the free subject in Kant's *Critique of Judgment*: the subject is liberated by making its own rules for aesthetic judgment and above all for artistic production. Aesthetic autonomy is the autonomy of genius. The critique of ideology then reconstructs the underlying social conditions of advanced division of labor, the alienating results of which cause the suffering of the romantic aesthetic subject, but are simultaneously the enabling condition of the subject's aesthetic independence. Inherent in anarchism is the image of a social subjectivity becoming at one with itself and no longer needing the heteronomous leadership of an avant-garde willing what is best for a liberated people.

Adorno argues against giving up, under any circumstances, the diagnosis, both clinical and utopian, provided by autonomous art in its radically alienating gestalt as high modernism. This is especially the case during later historical developments, which he describes in the 1930s and 1940s as the path to monopoly capitalist society, and in the 1960s as the "administered society" of late capitalism. Thus in his correspondence with Benjamin he acknowledges that the specific ideological critique of his aesthetics inclines him toward bourgeois romanticism, insofar as it carries on the dialectic of individuality in bourgeois society. Adorno's reflections in the prologue to *Minima Moralia* confirm this thinking: in the era of the individual's objective liquidation as social and philosophical category, the individual's cognitive potential can once again attain its full power. Equally active are the traces of early romanticism in his *Aesthetic Theory*. In that work, every form of reconciliation between the aesthetic and existing reality is rejected. That is as true for the "harmonious" reconciliation offered by idealist philosophy or popular culture as it is for the "extorted appeasement" of realism. The fragment is defined as the only authentic form still viable in the present. Texts by Kafka or Beckett are read not as existential statements but rather as ironic manifestations of the paradoxes of the precarious subject within an objectivity wholly defined by alienation.

The basic assumption of Adorno's aesthetics is that art is unconscious historiography. It is most authentically so when it withdraws from society's monopolizing grasp. Both visual art and music did this in the twentieth century by marking the boundaries between themselves and mass cultural art in the age of its technical reproducibility. The pathos of distance in abstract painting and atonal, serial music was the pathos of dissonant noncooperation in the mechanical representation of the real, to which photography was bound by images, and entertainment music by tonality, harmony, and rhythm. Adorno speaks of the two halves of freedom as a whole. Neither half is to be rendered absolute, but he decides for the half that is embodied in autonomous art. He does not declare it absolute, but demonstrates its underlying dialectic. Moreover, he negates the other half, art that is not autonomous but is bound to a [commercial] purpose. In order for this negation to appear more plausible than it really is, he declares the "consumer art" of modernity to be purely a product of manipulation.

Before the rise of the culture industry, this art had a relatively justified existence. By maintaining a certain retardation, either as craft or as a structure enhancing pleasure and public amusement, consumer art provided a negative index of truth: it documented the failure of high culture that repressed ordinary human existence. In their negative truth, however, the nonautonomous arts were always afflicted by the stigma of being valid not in themselves, but only in the reactive perspective of the cultural critic. And now they had completely forfeited even this residual truth, having become the deliberately circulated false coinage of the system of social delusion. To Adorno, it is unthinkable that systemically applied or functional arts, whether before or during the age of the culture industry, could possess their own genuine claim to validity and truth. But this claim is not really plausible. Modes of art can have legitimate functions without thereby being reduced to the status of ideological instruments. Adorno's strongest argument is that, whereas artworks of the past were sometimes *also* commodities, products of the culture industry are *nothing but* commodities. Technical reproducibility generates copies in massive numbers and permits massive circulation. Historical investigation of modern mass culture confirms this view. "Film was a commodity, produced as a standardized item for the purpose of maximizing profits. . . . Already before the First World War film production was economically concentrated and technically rationalized. . . . As soon as a successful formula seemed to be achieved, products were standardized in order to minimize costs and to make use of studios and photocopy shops in a genuinely industrial way" [Kasper Maase]. As Adorno sees it, questions of aesthetic truth content could no longer play any appropriate role. However, it should have become clear, at least since the ambitious products of "New Hollywood," that even within the film industry aesthetic achievements are possible that could not happen anywhere else.

The Work of Art and the Concept of Truth

For Adorno, it is in art that a reality truly in need of redemption becomes manifest. The truth of art is concretized only in individual works of art, and in these particular works, truth content appears through negation. Adorno sees art as the unconscious writing of history, making possible the unrestricted expression of the suffering of history's subject by mediating this expression through the opposite pole to mimetic expression, namely, through the rational construction of a work in accordance with its formal autonomy. Artworks display the real, but to the extent they are true artworks, they always do so in light of what could actually come to pass. As Albrecht Wellmer summarizes, "If one were to separate out analytically what Adorno thinks of as a dialectical unity, one could differentiate 'truth one' (aesthetic coherence) from 'truth two' (objective truth). The unity of these two factors means that art can express cognition of reality (truth two) only by means of aesthetic synthesis (truth one)—and, conversely, that aesthetic synthesis (truth one) can succeed only if reality (truth two) is made manifest through its agency."

The demand for philosophical experience that is open to "public truth," and does not ignore, by skimming over it or retreating mystically into the self, the "reality" that *does* disguise "public truth"—this demand finds its counterpart, and surely also its model, in the concept of aesthetic experience. In Adorno's thinking the stress on aesthetic subjectivity correlates with the residual objectivism of his truth concept.[5] In the concept of the authentic artwork—authentic through its historically mediated truth content—Adorno integrates motifs recalling Lukács's theory of tradition with motifs from Benjamin's negative philosophy of history. In his *Aesthetic Theory*, Adorno writes that the truth content of great artworks of the past never simply becomes obsolete, even when their claim to validity appears to have been negated by the ongoing development of autonomous art or when their "formal content" has been rendered antiquated by procedural innovations. Their claim to validity persists, albeit in a different way.

Benjamin developed the categories of "formal content" and "truth content" in his interpretation of Goethe's *Elective Affinities*. They function for him in relation to the perspective that revolutionary historical consciousness would consist in "rescuing" those elements of spiritual constructs that—wrongly presented—could not, in their original sociohistorical situation, actualize their potential. For Benjamin, then, revolutionary cultural consciousness would not be the tabula rasa mentality of rootless philistines demanding a "new beginning." Rather, it would appropriate alienated aesthetic contents in its own way, thereby under certain circumstances attaining for them their own authenticity, their own truth. In this, Benjamin's concept of a truth content to be rescued after the revolution differs from Lukács's idea that the victorious proletariat would, by reflecting on its contradictions, absorb into its identity the progressive contents of canonical bourgeois artworks. These contradictions had, according to Lukács, prevented their producers from transcending their false class consciousness.[6] A contemporary example suggests what this could mean. One can describe the dissolution of East Germany as a revolution: the philosophers Jürgen Habermas and Ulrich Sonneman argued this, in contrast to the Stalinist poet Peter Hacks, for whom the turn (*Wende*) was a "counterrevolution." In principle, then, three "postrevolutionary" ways of analyzing East German visual art are possible. One can regard East German painting indiscriminately as socialist-realist propaganda art, that is, as a counterpart to the programmatically abstract art of the West, standing in the antimodern, totalitarian tradition of conformist art from Nazi times. This position was taken by a 1999 exhibition of Weimar art, beset by scandals, titled "Rise and Fall of Modernity." It expresses a mentality of "liquidation," blind to all nuance. But one can also view individual works of official East German painting, such as Willi Sitte's disturbing portraits, as successful efforts to make tangible deviant experiences that could find their artistic home only after political liberation. This home would be a free art world, where the peculiar ways artists translate their experiences into formal structures are valued as the highest form of aesthetic logic. That would be a postsocialist version of Lukács's theory of tradition. From the perspective of Benjamin-style "rescue," the issue looks different again. Individual works, such as Werner Tübke's monumental panoramic images of the Peasants' Revolt, could be read ex post facto as monadic expressions of discontinuous experience, marking ruptures in the official historical story of homogeneous proletarian advance. In this way the early, genuinely mass-cultural panoramic form is revived by Tübke and put into practice at the highest level of craftsmanship, in a provocatively old-fashioned, objective, painterly mode. This process enacts a statement directed against both the anti-avant-garde dogmas of East Germany and the neo-avant-garde practices of the West: in a sense this is a genuine, East German postmodernism whose constructive power, as the self-parody of an aesthetic gesture adopted by the ruling class, can fully reveal itself only after the destruction of the conditions in which it was generated, to the extent that it is not seen merely as a picturesque ruin or a scurrilous marginal phenomenon. In Benjamin's words: "The critic asks about the truth content of an artwork, about what is alive in it, about truth as such." To the extent the artwork is understood by its later interpreters as a historical event, it is transformed. For Benjamin, the concept that was to "brush history against the grain" was not historical empathy but materialist-rational "mindfulness." Sven Kramer summarized this as follows: "Memory and historical writing can actualize and release the unused potentials of the past, and, by rescuing them, they formulate claims upon the future." Benjamin conceived these claims messianically; in the *Theses on the Philosophy of History*, he wrote, "The past carries with it a secret index, through which it is referred to redemption." This redemption would unleash the unbroken power of the collective cultural memory: "Only redeemed mankind gains full access to its past. That means that only for redeemed mankind has its past become, in every one of its moments, available for citation."

Adorno places similar reflections at the center of his aesthetics, although he largely empties them of messianic content, thereby maintaining a distance that keeps them secure against any temptation to work toward a new religion of art. The truth content of "authentic art of the past," he argues in *Aesthetic Theory*, does not die because of historical transformations within aesthetics: "A liberated humanity should receive the heritage of its antiquity for which it has atoned. What was once true in an artwork—and has been denied by the course of history—can only reveal itself again when the conditions are changed, because of which that truth had to be annulled: so deeply are history and truth content aesthetically intertwined."

What does this claim mean? I will try to explain it briefly, using, in Adorno's spirit, a musical example. Mozart's music fulfilled the strict formal logic of Viennese classicism. It could articulate only those expressive figures contained by this form, while others, such as dissonance, had to remain outside its territory. Thus the formal musical law of *The Magic Flute* expresses freedom of feeling and articulates the theme of erotic pleasure in a hitherto unknown shape. This expression is possible, however, only through the suppression of all expressive figures that do not fit the formal schema. The madness of pleasure that breaks all boundaries could not be articulated until Wagner's music, which begins to shatter the limits of tonality. In *Tannhäuser* the destructive and antisocial power of eros becomes tangible; in *Tristan and Isolde* the proximity of eros to death insists on being heard. Here, too, one kind of expression is possible only at the cost of repressing something else; with Wagner the ideology of the total work of art, as trace of the power of the whole, dominates his art down to its most intensely inward elements. We can conclude from this that if artists could one day be free of the need to prove their authenticity by incorporating into their works' formal structure the negativity of a world order that reached in Auschwitz its provisional high, or rather low, point, they might perhaps be freed from the mandate of dissonance. They would no longer have to withdraw from communication with their listeners; rather, they could actualize a communality between structural requirements and the need for vital reception, of which even today we still know nothing. The happy balance between high and mass art, which according to Adorno was realized in *The Magic Flute* for a brief, quickly vanishing moment, could return at a new level if Mozart were no longer the favorite of a ritualized class of music and Wagner no longer a canonical source (mediated via Erich Korngold to Hollywood) of film music. Then what Adorno noted about musical modernity would perhaps no longer be the case: "There is more pleasure in dissonance than consonance." The person who truly enjoys music, who experiences it not only intellectually but also, perhaps only, hedonistically, would no longer be in a state of untruth. "Reconciled reality and the restored element of truth in the past might well converge with each other," Adorno speculates. "The great works are waiting."

What are they waiting for? For Judgment Day? For the end of times? For a world revolution that succeeds after all, without cultural revolution and without show trials? Adorno's *negative* apocalyptic perspective in the field of aesthetics binds aesthetics indissolubly to the philosophy of history. Its aporia is a theory of revolution, and it underlies his reflections on the necessity and possibilities of modern art's evolving process to the point of its self-cancellation in Thomas Mann's *Doktor Faustus*. This is the negative philosophy of history from *Dialectic of Enlightenment*, according to which only "a mindfulness of nature within the subject, in the fulfillment of which is contained the whole truth of all culture" could break the spell confining Western culture. The West's irrational (measured against humane goals) rationality needs to be "redeemed," as Adorno sees it, through reconciliation with its historical antagonist, mimetic-expressive behavior, whereby life makes itself virtually identical with other life. Only consciously aesthetic behavior of this kind, in Adorno's view, could modify the abstractly standardizing, compulsory character of categorical reason in the administered world. Adorno's cognitive utopia consists in the reversal of the philosophical articulation of "totalized negativity" into its mirror image, the text of "its opposite": a text that, as theology puts it, is to be read in a "messianic light." "Cognition has no light but the one shining on the world from the source of redemption": this light, as it is phrased in *Minima Moralia*, makes the world appear "distorted and needy." Art that is a form of cognition and philosophy that opens itself toward the experience of "the open": these are Adorno's models. In Albrecht Wellmer's words, they are models for a "nonviolent bridging of the gap between perception and concept, between particular and general, between part and whole."

This definition of art's truth content in modernity omits certain aspects of aesthetic experience. The commitment to the philosophy of history reduces art to the developmental path on which it defines itself as autonomous art. This definition amputates not only all avant-garde art that moves beyond the limits of "the work," beyond the compulsion to organize (for example) musical material, such as the music of John Cage or Morton Feldman. It also excludes all varieties of applied art and mass art. In *Dialectic of Enlightenment*, Adorno and Horkheimer argue that "cinema, radio, jazz, and magazines" (a peculiar mixture of categories of form, genre, and media) are nothing but components of the "system of the culture industry." For Adorno, music was exclusively the kind produced by composers; improvised music, or music that sees its role as functional, such as dance music, appears merely as the noise of advertising or the background murmur of the culture industry.

The story is the same for art's communicative accomplishments, which Adorno wholly rejects; like Horkheimer, Adorno was convinced that all authentic art, at least since the high point of classical modernity, refuses communication with human beings in order to announce silently that, within the catastrophic reality, understanding must be a lie. Two aspects of this assumption, however, are controversial. First, "communication" is here reduced to the goal of reaching agreement, to intentions that for Adorno belong in the realm of the commercial and the conformist—whereas "communication" in reality can mean all possible varieties of interaction. Second, it is not true that artworks portraying human terrors and sufferings—such as Picasso's *Guernica* or Kafka's and Beckett's depictions of failed understanding—would not *communicate* the terror, the suffering, and the failure to communicate. But Adorno has to cut these aspects out of his argument in order to illuminate the gap between "actuality" and "authentic art" with the vividness he desires.

Even (or especially) the concept of truth in aesthetics is, for Adorno, structured in a utopian-transcendental way. Truth is conceived not as free-floating, but as a point of alignment, to be defined intellectually, for the possibility of fusing cognition and praxis in the world as it is. It is the criterion for making distinctions, whereby Adorno differentiates his philosophical project from the presumably inadequate philosophy that remains purely "technical," purely "reconstructive." Is this differentiation persuasive? Adorno's insistence that philosophy must achieve more and different things than mere persuasion through arguments cannot absolve his theory of truth from confronting arguments that test its validity claim. For how could the sufficient condition for a philosophy's ambitious claims be fulfilled, if the necessary condition is lacking?

Adorno constructs an opposition between conceptual rationality and mimetic expression that cannot be overcome through mediation, so long as there is no practical "redemption" from the heteronomy of a law of social operation that appears to be a law of nature. Wellmer criticizes this with an argument of communication theory deriving from Habermas: because Adorno's thinking remains enclosed within the paradigm of the philosophy of consciousness, he is able to conceptualize cognition only through a subject-object antithesis; in order to access the perspective of "redemption," he must reach back into an extraterritorial "other" of rationality (borrowed from Ludwig Klages). Wellmer argues that Adorno could not see the mimetic moment within rationality itself, in its structure of communicative interaction that has understanding as its goal. This is true to the extent that Adorno simply did not trust analytic philosophy to gain access to the potential that, in his view, could only begin to approach the truth of "things in themselves" by means of a constellatory language. Moreover, Adorno operated with a peculiarly narrow concept of communication. But it is incorrect to claim that Adorno sought to summon mimetic strengthening *from outside*. In his dialectical theory, there is no "outside," as Wellmer stresses. "Mimesis . . . as the other of rationality" is always already its own *other*. And, as Wellmer puts it, Adorno would in no way "think the coming together of mimesis and rationality only as a negation of historical reality," since he did not conceive of it simply as negating historical reality, but rather as the *defined negation* of a defined form of *historical praxis*, a negation that, for now, we are able to grasp most readily with the help of messianic-transcendental allegories—so long as it does not take practical shape as active negation.

8

The Failure of Culture

THE CENTRAL THOUGHT IN Adorno's critical theory of culture is formulated in *Minima Moralia*: "that culture has failed until now is no justification for reinforcing its failure." It was always the culturally critical standpoint of critical theory that gained a broad public reception in the postwar era. And the theme of culture is again very current in today's debates: cultural sciences, culturalist theories of society, and political programs of multiculturalism are all on a rising trend.

Traditionally, culture was defined, in the words of Jakob Burckhardt, as "the sum of those spiritual developments that occur spontaneously and do not claim universal or mandatory validity." In contrast to today's current, functionalist understanding of culture as a human community marked by continuity of experience, behavior, and way of thinking, Burckhardt's definition aims at an objective concept of culture, focused on the essence of the object to be defined. At the same time, however, Burckhardt stresses culture's function : the satisfaction of human beings' material and spiritual needs. He points out that we can never quite separate the material and spiritual elements of culturally shaped behavior. And he articulates a basic idea of modern sociotheoretical understanding of culture: the "total form" of culture "in relation to state and religion is society in the broadest sense." This materialistically tinged conception of culture still aspires to wholeness: it claims to be able to deliver a closed definition of culture's essence. With this move Burckhardt has simultaneously leaped ahead of the now tired-sounding differentiation between culture and civilization, which became established after his time and remained for a long time normative for twentieth-century philosophical cultural critique. Today's discussion has gone beyond this frankly idealistic labeling of culture and civilization, separating these concepts from the social. However, the problem of a philosophical concept of culture remains. Today's dominant relativist image of culture is in fact self-contradictory. Herbert Schnädelbach formulated the issue thus: the relativist concept of culture is sustained by

> [the] conviction that culture as such exists only in a variety of cultures: in the Western, the Chinese, the Hopi-variant, etc. At this point the questions begin concerning the unity of culture, cultural universals, and the undesired side effects of cultural relativism; whoever dares to defend ideas of unity and generality is subjected without fail to the suspicion of Western imperialist ethnocentrism. It is amazing that such pluralism grows precisely at the same rate that world culture moves toward planetary networking and normativity.

The Radically Pathetic and Guilty Culture

Understanding the uniformity of modern culture and its inner contradictions was a central theme for Adorno. No aspect of his thinking has resonated so strongly in society's consciousness as his dialectical theory of culture—and at the same time, none has been so frequently misunderstood. There are two likely causes for this: the lifelong intensity with which Adorno dedicated himself to the theme, and the inner ambivalence of the object, culture, that he sought to reconstruct dialectically. The insistence with which Adorno turned again and again to cultural phenomena and the social structures underlying them heightened the presence of his thinking in the magazines and the cultural sections of the mass media—something unusual for a philosopher, but characteristic of his impact. But the dialectical tension that Adorno's theory brought to culture's internal contradictions was generally not pursued in the magazines.

Adorno confronted the questionable quality of the cultural operations restored after the Second World War with the rupture of civilization that had taken place in the concentration camp system. In his eyes, this rupture embodied not the "other" of culture but the outcome of a catastrophic intensification of what is always already present as an element of culture: domination over nature. Yet this thought was largely misunderstood as an isolated judgment concerning the end of culture, instead of being placed in its proper dialectical context.

This misreading is apparent in the fate of that famous dictum in Adorno's 1955 collection, *Prisms*: "to write a poem after Auschwitz is barbaric." Even now this sentence is often read as if its author wanted to proclaim an excommunication. Detlev Claussen has probed the history of this misunderstanding. He has shown how Adorno's remark has been interpreted to this day as a kind of negative-theological commandment, as if he had proclaimed "Thou shalt not write a poem after Auschwitz." This view can be reinforced by a sentence from *Negative Dialectics*, published eleven years after *Prisms*: "All culture after Auschwitz . . . is garbage." This statement can be read as a devastating judgment, as a negative definition of the essence of all cultural and civilizational efforts and achievements, whereby a radical negativist pulls the rug out from under his own critique without being troubled by this logical inconsistency. A spirit that always says no, and takes pleasure in denying the social basis of its own activity—for what did Adorno do but "cultural work"?—such a spirit could have a reputation for writerly brilliance, but could hardly be seen as "philosophically consistent." But what was and is overlooked in making such a judgment is precisely dialectics—the very lifeblood of the sentence from *Minima Moralia* cited at the start of this chapter. "That culture has failed until now" simply means that it has not yet become fully real. The failure of culture is, for Adorno, not merely something imposed from outside. The "relapse into barbarism" that occurred in

Auschwitz, which persists "as long as the conditions enabling that relapse essentially endure," has something to do with culture itself. In Adorno's view, the traditional concept of culture is often defined by the exclusion of nature, thereby making domination of nature into an absolute. Yet it also has a hidden side: the utopia of release from the sheer compulsion to dominate nature, of the comprehensive humanization of being in the form of a reconciliation with nature. But this submerged content first has to be fortified against the dominant concept of culture. Thus Adorno does not simply throw overboard the humanist-bourgeois concept of culture, but, rather, adopts its liberating prospect of a genuinely human life for everyone as his own project.

Adorno thus advocates solidarity with culture at the very moment when its historical failure is unmistakable. The dictum about Auschwitz is inevitably misunderstood if it is detached from this intellectual framework and handed down in isolation. Here is Adorno's full context:

> the more society is totalized, the more spirit is reified—and the more paradoxical the enterprise becomes for spirit to free itself from reification through its own strength. Even the most intense consciousness of destiny is liable to degenerate into prattle. Cultural critique is faced by the ultimate stage of the dialectic between culture and barbarism: to write a poem after Auschwitz is barbaric—and that also eats away at the understanding that tells us why it became impossible to write poems today. So long as the critical spirit remains cocooned in self-satisfied contemplation, it is not up to the task of confronting the absolute reification which took for granted spiritual progress as one of its elements—and today is on the point of swallowing it up absolutely.[1]

For Adorno what is involved here is the philosophical aporia of cultural critique. Self-sufficient philosophy, spirit that remains in its own world, can no longer conceive of an authentic version of humanly appropriate existence in late capitalist society after Auschwitz. As he puts it, spirit cannot, "on its own terms, elude" commodification. Philosophical cultural criticism fails as an immanent critique of culture because it asserts as absolute a normative standard that is itself drenched in what is seen, from the perspective of an idealist understanding of culture, as the antithesis of culture: violence and repression. Conservative cultural critique claims to defend the "values" of culture—understood as purely spiritual—against its supposed decay. But by binding culture to values that are hypostasized as absolute even as they lose any dynamic relation to the social framework of life, this critique involuntarily turns values into the opposite of what they should be.

Cultural values that are divorced from the reality of the division of labor evidently accommodate themselves smoothly to barbaric practices. In the evening the commandant of the concentration camp provides enjoyment for himself and his colleagues through musical performances, and the earth does not automatically open to swallow him up; this enables one to gauge what culture will tolerate. Conservative cultural critique, by averting its gaze from culture's dark sides, becomes committed to the "culture as alibi" which Max Frisch diagnosed in Germany in 1949. Ten years later, Adorno speaks in the same vein:

> The concept of culture, in German linguistic usage, is defined exclusively as spiritual culture, in increasingly stark contrast with praxis. This mirrors the fact that the full emancipation of the bourgeoisie was unsuccessful or succeeded only at a moment when bourgeois society could no longer be equated with humanity. The failure of the revolutionary movements that sought, in the Western countries, to actualize the concept of culture as freedom, drove the ideas of those movements back in on themselves, not only obscuring the link between them and the project of actualizing them, but imposing a taboo on them. Culture became self-sufficient, indeed ultimately, in the language of worn-out philosophy, a "value" per se. We are indebted to this self-sufficiency for major speculative metaphysics and the great music that is at one with it in its innermost essence. At the same time, however, such spiritualization of culture virtually confirms its practical impotence; human beings' real lives are handed over to blindly persisting, blindly functioning social relations.

Thus, for Adorno, conservative, immanent cultural critique is afflicted because it helps to destroy what it wishes to preserve. Yet the opposite attitude is no better. The transcendent critique of culture from outside either argues for a bourgeois, conservative critique of culture in the name of life and nature or, representing a concept of class war, dismisses bourgeois culture in a lightning stroke as an empty, superstructural swindle. Both versions of the critique of culture are inadequate. In both cases, spiritual structures are draped in an abstract concept of ideology.

> With the logic of consistency and the pathos of truth . . . cultural criticism could demand that all social relations be rigorously reduced to their material basis, that they be ruthlessly and openly conceptualized according to the interests shaping the lives of those involved. . . . But if one wanted to act radically in accordance with this logic, one would eradicate, together with the untrue, everything that is true in this situation, everything that strives, however powerlessly, to escape the realm of universal praxis, every chimerical anticipation of a more noble condition—and one would pass without mediation into the very barbarism with which, in its mediated form, one reproaches mainstream culture. This reversal was always a possibility among bourgeois cultural critics after Nietzsche: Spengler endorsed it enthusiastically. But Marxists are not inoculated against it.[2]

If the critique of ideology is pursued within the frame of an abstract negation of the truth element that is always also present within the seeming autonomy of cultural phenomena, then, for Adorno, it is itself ideological: a necessarily false social consciousness, not the higher truth of an accurate class perspective.

To grasp the aporia of cultural criticism means, for Adorno, that one must resist the alternative of "putting culture as a whole in question, using the master category of ideology, or confronting it with the norms that culture itself crystallized out." But Adorno avoids this alternative, not by constructing a completely different third critical perspective, but by rejecting the either-or dichotomy. Critical theory wants both: it combines the approaches and allows them to correct each other. It does not embrace culture as something purely spiritual, as ultimate essence, because that would mean that "despair and infinite suffering," the real-life outcome of culture's failure, would be idealistically transfigured. But it also rejects the relativist weakening of cultural and spiritual claims to truth and validity by means of an abstract critique of ideology. Adorno sees the two antithetical viewpoints as symptoms of spiritual reification. That is, both freeze a reactive definition and turn it into an absolute, whereas only the dialectical interweaving of both viewpoints could do justice to the ambivalence of culture itself. That is why Adorno terms it paradoxical when spirit seeks "to free itself from reification through its own strength." Spirit that is true to its identity, that fulfills its purpose—that of trying to grasp things as they are—implicates itself, by becoming more actively contemplative, in the wretched truth that culture has become the way it now is.

Adorno's "dialectic turn of cultural critique" thus envisions the transition from theory to practice—practice that cannot generate thinking from within itself. The premise is thinking that neither idolizes culture as pure truth nor rejects it as a lie. The latter risk is one of greater concern for Adorno, as it probably is for most of us today. For today culture seems to cancel itself out through the very universality of its impact, since its critical contents are increasingly placed in the service of maintaining the processes of commodity production. Moreover, stale idealistic culture worship continues to live on underground in the renaissance of the culturalist social theories that characterized the sociotheoretical discourse of the 1990s. As an explicit position, however, it is no longer taken seriously anywhere. All the more urgent for critical theory, then, becomes a solidarity with culture's hidden truth content. "To identify culture exclusively with falsehood is especially fateful at the moment when culture really does turn wholly into falsehood, and energetically enforces such an identification in order to compromise every resistant idea": here Adorno clearly stresses the positive side of culture, which consists in refusing a total submission to the law of commodity production, exchange value, thereby offering a continuing link to the perspective of a society liberated from commodity rule.

> If we define material reality as the world of exchange value, but define culture as whatever refuses to accept the domination of that value, then, to be sure, such refusal lacks impact so long as things remain the same. However, since the notion of free and just exchange is actually

the real lie, then whatever denies it is de facto a voice for truth: in the face of the lie of the commodity world, the voice denouncing it becomes a corrective, even if it is itself a lie. That culture has failed until now is no justification for reinforcing its failure.

As outlined above, the exchange principle of bourgeois capitalist society is a lie, because its basis is the unfair distribution of property, which allows the freedom to exploit other human beings to coexist with the compulsion to sell one's labor as a commodity and therefore always be cheated out of its full value. To the extent that culture retains the notion that there must be a value not subject to the exchange principle, this truth, however falsely clothed, represents the insight that culture and society must be subjected to dialectical analysis.

Adorno writes, "The dialectically minded critic of culture must both participate in culture and withdraw from it. Only then can he be just toward both culture and himself." Adorno thus claims that, although critical theory is indeed a part of its own culture, it is simultaneously entitled to assume a position external to it from which it can practice critique. Here, too, Münchhausen's trick would have to be implemented. Yet Adorno knows that there is no salvation; although cultural constructs are not pure truth, neither is the critique of them, since that critique appears merely as an intellectual construct even when it is dialectical. To act as if culture could simply be continued after Auschwitz is false, hence Adorno's opinion that it "became impossible to write poems today." Moreover, the merely theoretical insight into this situation is similarly false, hence his comment that "the very expression of this insight gets eaten away." But dialectical understanding is all we have, so long as there is no transformative social praxis. Thus, "the failure of culture must not be reinforced." Moreover, the right of subjective suffering to express itself subjectively is not negated by either the aporias of culture or the critique of culture: "Whatever could be called culture, without overtones of cliché, intended, as an expression of suffering and contradiction, to hold on to the idea of a just life." Later, in *Negative Dialectics*, Adorno developed this thought as a self-correction of his statement in *Prisms*—a correction, however, that in another sense intensifies the statement. "Perennial suffering has as much right to expression as the martyr has to cry out; thus it may have been wrong to say that no poem could be written after Auschwitz. But the less 'cultural' question is not wrong: could life be lived after Auschwitz, could the survivor feel entitled to it, having escaped by chance, feeling that he should by right have been killed?" As an achievement of modern bourgeois society, culture is the bearer of a humane element. But in a society in transition to an authoritarian state, culture passes a quick judgment on itself. And post-totalitarian society is affected by this.

> All culture after Auschwitz, including the urgent critique of it, is garbage. By restoring itself along lines that offered no resistance in its sphere, culture has completely become the ideology that it potentially already was, ever since, in its opposition to material existence, it presumed to fill existence with the light that the separation of spirit from physical work withheld from it. Whoever advocates supporting this radically guilty and pathetic culture makes himself its enabler, while whoever rejects culture directly advances the barbarism which culture revealed itself to be. Not even silence helps one escape from this circle.

Yet there remains a hidden drive to bring a humane social order into being; for Adorno, this drive is the potential within the cultural for opposition to the hegemony of exchange value. Elsewhere he speaks of the related power of awareness of the cultural, a power that works to enhance a perspective of reconciliation between nature and culture, as well as between the particular and the general in society: "Whatever is justifiably called cultural is driven to remember and activate what is discarded during that process of ongoing domination of nature, mirrored in growing rationality and ever more rational means of control. Culture is the perennial objection of the particular against the general, so long as the general remains unreconciled with the particular."

Enlightenment as Mass Deception

If, however, the universal principle of exchange value takes control of culture as a whole, then the perspectival power of resistance is lost. Culture no longer strengthens the socially particular against the general, but becomes the instrument for consummating the latter. Culture's self-negation, whereby it continues on in its new robes as a false, affirmative culture, is something Adorno and Horkheimer investigated during their American exile, as an outcome of an international social phenomenon: the culture industry. Kurt Lenk writes,

> Far from indulging in a European superiority complex vis-à-vis America in this respect, Adorno sees early on that, in this tendency toward ruthless and totalized commercialization, America is only a few steps ahead of Europe. As long as social control was not total, in prefascist Europe, a consciousness of relative spiritual autonomy, even if utopian, could develop in the corners of a cultural realm not yet completely dominated by the law of commodity exchange. With the concentration of the economy and state administration, however, these relicts are lost.

In the chapter of *Dialectic of Enlightenment* devoted to the culture industry, the authors explore this most advanced stage of cultural dialectics, and describe it as a manifestation of the struggle of modern reason with itself. The spread of the culture industry is a negative indicator of what cultures have in common, previously discussed in relation to the humanizing mission of culture as a whole. For critical theory, the culture industry is the mask of the idea of a universal human culture, the mocking caricature of the program of the Enlightenment—which itself played a role in producing it.

Adorno defines the concept of the culture industry, which has become one of critical theory's most effective legacies, in contradistinction to the term "mass culture." The culture industry engages all the same phenomena as "mass culture," namely, the forms of artistic and cultural production with a mass reception in the twentieth century: cinema, radio, print media, canned music, television. But just as folk music is not music of the people, but produced as music for the people, the products of the culture industry do not belong to the masses in the sense that they might use them to express themselves authentically and articulate their cultural needs—as Benjamin interpreted the art form of the film. Looking back from the 1960s, Adorno reports,

> In our drafts we used the term "mass culture." We replaced it with "culture industry" in order to exclude a priori the interpretation with which champions in the field are comfortable: that it is a matter of something like a culture rising spontaneously from the masses themselves, of our current image of folk art. Culture industry differs radically from this. It fuses old familiar things into a new quality. In all its branches, products are more or less consciously produced that are designed for consumption by the masses and, to a significant degree, determine this consumption themselves. Individual branches are structurally similar, or at least fit easily together. Almost seamlessly, they become part of the social system. That enables them to use both today's advanced technologies and the concentrated structure of the economy and administration.

Adorno stresses that "the expression 'industry' is not to be taken literally.... It refers to the standardization of the cultural entity itself—like the model of the Western familiar to every film audience—and to the rationalization of distribution techniques, but not strictly to the production process." The reception of the culture industry's products is accordingly shaped by preformed, standardized schemata of perception.

As Heinz Paetzold puts it, the core fact is "that in late capitalism a mechanism with vast consequences had arisen for integrating people into the existing social system. The trend to individualization is replaced by one toward stereotypical behavior. Instead of a liberation from work pressures in their free time, people are shaped by reflexes that repeat the work rhythm." In *Dialectic of Enlightenment*, Horkheimer and Adorno argue that perpetual sameness is the essence of the culture industry: "Culture today brands everything with similarity." "What is new about the mass cultural phase, in contrast with late liberalism, is the exclusion of the new." The appearance of this new era, however, is permanent upheaval, constant change of the supposedly newest products. Perpetual sameness looks like ceaseless change. Horkheimer and Adorno explain this, using critical economics, as the necessity of even speedier circulation of culture industry products: they can generate the profit mandated by cultural economics only if they are permanently up to date, according to the industry's immanent criteria. But the requirement of permanent circulation presupposes, in the realm of the culture industry, that products do not close themselves off from consumers' customary expectations. Only what follows familiar patterns has a chance of broad sales. Whoever cuts the pages of a detective novel, said Brecht, has very specific expectations, which he does not wish to see disappointed. Experts in the industry are recognizable by their talent for producing, with assured effectiveness, works that do not offend against any ingrained assumptions, yet do not seem monotonous. This alone decides the success of a culture industry product. Steven Spielberg's film about Oskar Schindler was a big success, while Claude Lanzmann's documentary film *Shoah*, which explored new ways of portraying memory, could not be. One cannot imagine the deadly serious, formally strict *Investigation* (1965) by Peter Weiss as a theatrical hit, the way Joshua Sobol's lively ghetto-revue was in the 1980s. Achieving the balance between the appearance of novelty and the tried and true is the crucial test of the culture industry.

It may sound paradoxical, but the critical theory of the culture industry is not primarily a "cultural critique." Rather, it is a critique of the commodity format in its most recent social manifestation. The issue is how to grasp the structural shift of a society that is rapidly transforming itself, by analyzing the sociocultural phenomena on its surface. In Adorno's historical, philosophical, and aesthetic theory of the new, articulated in *Minima Moralia*, he shows that these problems do not appear only with the culture industry's functionalization of the aesthetic, but are already present in the autonomous art of modernity. The dialectic of the modern, both in its socioeconomic modes of production and in its aesthetic emancipation, is grounded in the ambivalence of the new. In the modern aesthetics of Poe and Baudelaire, the idea of the new is phantasmagorical. This aesthetics rebels, in the name of something new—the experience of something other than what is—against the dominant tendency of bourgeois society and its busy production of commodities. But by doing so, this aesthetics remains under a curse: even the most innovative artwork, in its very openness to unique experience, necessarily participates in the general uniformity of the social life-form. "In the cult of the new, hence in the very idea of the modern, there is a rebellion against the absence of the new," Adorno writes.

> The perpetual sameness of manufactured goods, the network of socialization, that both captures and assimilates objects and ways of perceiving them, transforms everything freshly encountered into a reiteration of what is always already present, into a random example of a genre, into the double of an existing model. The level of the unanticipated . . . appears completely exhausted. The idea of the new dreams of this level. Itself unattainable, the new constitutes itself, in place of the fallen God, as the vision of the first full consciousness of the decay of experience. But the concept of the new remains under the spell of experience's sickness; its abstractness testifies to this, focused impotently on actualizing experience as it slips away.

When the new is praised abstractly as the essence upon which everything depends, then it can no longer be distinguished from the basic principle of commodity-producing society. The issue, for Adorno, is that the totality of false social life always quickly catches up with even the most advanced efforts to escape it, since it is necessarily reproduced in their formal structures. "Whatever flashes up, in contrast to relaxed perception which merely attains the socially pre-formed cast of things, is itself repetition. The new, when sought for its own sake, in a sense produced in the laboratory and hardened into a formula, becomes in its sudden manifestation the compulsive return of the old." In this context, therefore, Adorno finds the "discovery of the new" to be simultaneously "eternal return as curse." But that does not mean he is articulating an aesthetic ontology implying the fateful necessity of this eternal return. In the introspection of artists in recent modernity—in the case of Beckett, for example, a central figure for Adorno—the category of the new has itself become brittle. Insofar as Beckett's *Endgame* portrays the eternal return of the same as the inevitability of the absurd, it gives aesthetic form to "history's framework of blindness" even as it "smashes it with form as weapon." The cult of the new actually prevents the arrival of the new. But the radical portrayal of the absence of the new generates an empty space which the new could occupy.

Adorno does not simply reconstruct the culture industry as a danger threatening art from outside, but, as his use of the concept of the new makes clear, views it as emerging from the dialectic of modern art. Only by overlooking this point can one see Adorno as critiquing the (American) culture industry in a conservative manner from the bastion of the supposedly elite (European) culture. Contemporary defenders of certain elements in modern mass culture, who focus on the expansion of the scope of freedom and experience and believe that mass culture contributes to this expansion, have judged Adorno's relation to the culture industry in just this way, and thus have criticized it sharply or sought to relativize it ironically. Certainly Adorno had little understanding of mass culture's genuine achievements. For example, he perceived only two things about jazz: the seeming freedom of a rhythmic schematism that actually induced conformity and the stereotypical format of set pieces, out of which the soloists' improvisations are always assembled. Adorno's critique of jazz suffers from his ignoring all those forms that transcend that schematism productively—which existed from the outset—and acting as though his judgment could claim universal validity. On the other hand, although Adorno did not produce close readings of films as Siegfried Kracauer did, he generated the outline of an aesthetics of film as authentic art form, oriented toward classic works by Charlie Chaplin, or by Michelangelo Antonioni and Volker Schlöndorff in the 1960s. Here, unlike in *Dialectic of the Enlightenment*, Adorno differentiates between the monopoly of film by the culture industry and the objective aesthetic content of the medium. This difference is shortchanged in *Dialectic of the Enlightenment*, although there too the subversive power of the Marx Brothers films is stressed.

Adorno's critique of the culture industry is essentially concerned with something other than condemning supposedly substandard products of mass culture from the perspective of the cultivated bourgeoisie's normative aesthetics. To the contrary, Adorno stresses precisely that a significant resistance against the lie of established "high" culture cannot take place because the subversive potential of "low" forms such as amusement parks, fairs, and circuses is domesticated by the omnipresent culture industry and thus unable to exert its power of the absurd. It is wholly absorbed into the commodity-based rhythm of offering means of distraction designed to generate, in consumers' minds, conformity with the structure of existing society.

The crux of Adorno's critique is the experience of a different kind of loss. The partial autonomy of works of art, which in the nineteenth century was to be developed to the very limits of the possible, contains, in his view, an element of resistance against the functional rationality of bourgeois society. At the same time, the autonomy of art is made fully possible only through art's character as commodity, since it is only in bourgeois society that the artist gains the status of an independent player in the exchange market. The goods he has to sell are artworks. But what becomes lost in the culture industry is the immanent, aesthetic use value of the works. That does not mean that the products of the culture industry are no longer worth anything. In this context, the term "aesthetic use value" refers to the element in artworks that is more than their economic substratum. It is not "the commodity character of art that is new," Adorno says, but the fact that

> today it deliberately declares itself, and that art renounces its own autonomy, lining itself up proudly among the consumer goods: this is the appeal of novelty. Art as a separate realm was always possible only as bourgeois art. Even its freedom, definable as the negation of social functionalism imposed through the market, remains essentially tied to the assumptions of a commodity society. Pure artworks, negating society's commodity character solely by following their own law, were always also commodities: until the eighteenth century the protection of their clients guarded artists from the market, and for that very reason they were subordinate to their clients and their clients' purposes. The purposelessness of the more modern great artwork lives off the anonymity of the market. And the market's demands are mediated in such various ways that the artist remains, to a certain extent, free from any specific expectation; for to his autonomy, as something merely tolerated, was added, throughout the era of bourgeois society, an element of untruth—that finally developed into the social liquidation of art. The mortally ill Beethoven, hurling away a novel by Walter Scott with the cry, "The guy is just writing for money," while at the same time showing himself to be an experienced and stubborn busi-

nessman in financial dealings over his final quartets, those ultimate renunciations of the market: this juncture offers the most vivid example of the unity of opposites, market and autonomy, in bourgeois art. Ideology envelops precisely those who cover up the contradiction instead of consciously absorbing it into their own production process.[3]

Adorno is unyielding on this point. He refuses the aestheticizing dream of prebourgeois society, instead explaining this aestheticism through the sociology of art: aestheticism needs precisely the social base that it despises in its art. But Adorno registers critically the loss of tension which the culture industry inevitably brings with it: the tension between autonomy and commodity function is dissolved in favor of the latter.

> What is new about the culture industry is the direct, unconcealed primacy of what is, in its most typical products, a precisely calculated effect. The autonomy of artworks—which indeed hardly ever prevailed unambiguously and was always infiltrated by the contexts where it operated—is tending toward elimination by the culture industry, with or without the conscious cooperation of those involved . . . the overall practice of the culture industry copies the profit motive onto the very face of spiritual structures. . . . Spiritual structures in the style of the culture industry are no longer also commodities—they are commodities through and through.

The dialectic of art and that of culture are both silenced by the culture industry. Servicing the customer, whose satisfaction is promised, is in actuality the conscription of all consumers into a system of producing and exchanging commodities that cares little for the needs of individuals. "The customer is not king, as the culture industry would have you believe, is not its subject but its object," Adorno writes. The culture industry manipulates. The critical economic and social psychological aspects of Adorno's critique have the same sociotheoretical basis. It is the assumption, already discussed in the context of Adorno's theory of individuation, that bourgeois society, with its liberal market economy and the typical character types corresponding to it, is on the path of transformation into the "total society" of the authoritarian state. In this process the "ideological media" have the function of guiding and disciplining the "demoralized masses" according to the plans that "the captains," "the deciders" of the social production process have for them: "The culture industry is the deliberate integration of its buyers from above." This presupposes, in Adorno's view, the tendency toward a monopolistic economy, which he saw operating everywhere in the 1940s. "Today, as the free market draws to an end," that is, "under monopoly structures," there is now only a "pseudomarket." In the 1960s he reformulated his views and abandoned the claim that the contemporary capitalism of the developed industrial states was a monopolist, authoritarian state capitalism that had banished competition and circulation. Even after this change, however, Adorno continued to ground his thinking in the manipulative character of the culture industry. As he saw it, nobody actually believed in the quality and truth of the culture industry's standard products, but their sheer presence, their distribution, and their omnipresent impact signaled the weight and seeming immutability of the existing social condition.

The "tone of ironic tolerance" adopted by many intellectuals today, much more than in Adorno's time, in order to make their peace with the "anything goes" attitude of the "new media," does not do justice to the issue. Even if the assumptions of monopolistic market liquidation and purposefully directed manipulation of the masses, which made sense in the 1940s, can no longer be applied to current developments in this field, Adorno's analysis remains valid in its essential features. Viewed economically, today's culture industry is characterized not by the development of monopolies but certainly by intensified concentration of capital. If Warner Bros. in the 1940s seemed threatened by the development of television—bringing film "into people's apartments on the model of radio"—then today, reborn as Time Warner, it fights very effectively, against few competitors, for the dominant share of the home video and DVD market. They and their comrades in arms are in the process of covering the United States and the whole world with the data highway, serving their own economic and strategic interests and satisfying consumers' needs only as a side effect. From a social-psychological perspective, "vicarious satisfaction" of needs is still offered, while dullness, uniformity, and the provision of disconnected clichés are invoked as "experience," "action," and "humor." Berlin's "Love Parades," global commercial television, or worldwide media spectacles derived from sports or music: the culture industry generates products that appear as new but actually remain the same. Thus it cooperates in producing the "dependence and enslavement of human beings" within a social totality that it itself produces, but which appears as a relationship of nature. "The categorical imperative of the culture industry, unlike that of Kant, no longer has anything in common with freedom. It states: thou shalt fit in, without knowing into what; fit into what already exists, into whatever everyone thinks anyway, as a reaction to the system's power and omnipresence." To that extent, "the overall impact of the culture industry is that of an anti-Enlightenment; in it, enlightenment, namely, the ongoing technical domination of nature, becomes mass deception, a means of imprisoning consciousness. It blocks the development of autonomous, independent individuals who could make conscious judgments and decisions." Adorno reaches a dark conclusion: "If one understands culture with sufficient urgency as the de-barbarization of human beings, lifting them out of the primitive state without perpetuating that state through violent repression, then culture has altogether failed. It has not been able to migrate into human beings, so long as the preconditions of a humane existence are lacking."

Jean-François Lyotard has described, vividly and specifically, the cultural-industrial face of the eclecticism of a "weakened postmodernity," which he rejects, thereby pointing toward its social causes.

> You listen to reggae, see Westerns, eat lunch at McDonald's, and enjoy home cooking at night; you wear French perfume in Tokyo, dress nostalgically in Hong Kong, and have an insight into the question posed by the TV quiz. It is easy to find a public for eclectic works. By turning into kitsch, art flatters the confusion that rules the "taste" of its fans. Artist, gallery owner, critic, and public: all delight in sheer randomness; it is the age of weakening standards. But this realism of the random is a realism of money: in the absence of aesthetic criteria it is both possible and useful to measure the value of works by their profitability. This realism can be adapted to all trends, like capital, which adapts itself to all "needs"—with the indispensable proviso that trends and needs dispose of the necessary purchasing power.[4]

The end of art in the business of the culture industry would be a potential "destruction of art." On this point one may assume Adorno and Lyotard would have agreed. But Adorno's diagnosis goes still further with the assertion that this destruction of art is not only possible but is actually becoming a reality in the second half of the twentieth century: "While the situation no longer permits art—that was the core of the statement about the impossibility of poems after Auschwitz—it still needs art. For the vision-free reality is the perfect counterpoint of the vision-free condition in which art would disappear, because the utopia that is encoded in every artwork would have become a reality. In itself, art is incapable of such an end." Art is oriented toward revolutionary social praxis, shaped by theoretical reflection about a liberated, self-determined condition.

Meanwhile, critical discourse about mass culture has become less dramatic. This is made clear by the variants of critical theory concerning mass and everyday culture that have been put forward by the English-speaking scholars. Two examples are Fredric Jameson's theory of the dialectic of ideology and utopia in the commodified reification of the visual unconscious and the reception aesthetics of cultural studies. Jameson's reading of the critique of the culture industry stresses its sociological foundations in the comparison of cultures. When the authors of *Dialectic of Enlightenment* formulated their theory of the culture industry, the American cultural sector was becoming wholly accessible to monopoly capitalism, while reactionary Germany was terrorizing Europe with its outdated petit bourgeois revolution. On the one hand, Jameson argues, *Dialectic of Enlightenment* continued the genre of modern European travel literature, which subjects North American democracy and its political, social, and cultural forms to comparative criticism. On the other hand, *Dialectic of Enlightenment* insisted on a structural "indissociability of the Culture Industry and fascism," contending that the difference between bourgeois-capitalist and authoritarian state structure is merely a gradual one. For Jameson, that has been the sting of *Dialectic of Enlightenment* in all subsequent critical discourses theorizing culture: the book showed "the identification of mass culture and the commodity form" to be a totalitarian paradigm of modern mass society—

and became the indispensable "basis for a cultural critique of capitalism itself" in North America to the present day.

The difference between Jameson's and Adorno's critiques of the culture industry consists in the way Jameson highlights the extent to which avant-garde and mass culture are related and dialectically interdependent. Jameson sees them as the two forms of capitalism's divided aesthetic production. In capitalism's present multinational stage, the classical-modern problem of the dualism between high and mass culture persists, indeed intensifies, because it is no longer a problem of our subjective criteria of judgment but a socially based contradiction. As Jameson sees it, mass culture, which has absorbed into itself the older popular art and culture, colonizes the visual unconscious in postmodern capitalist society; it is shaped into forms that are analogous to commodity form and compatible with it. But the products of mass culture are not wholly absorbed into "commodification"—the commodity-shaped reification of the collective unconscious and preconscious. They have also an expressive function, which aesthetically transforms social and political fears and fantasies. Products of mass culture manage these fears and fantasies; often, if not most of the time, they suppress or repress them. But for this suppression to succeed, these fears and fantasies must first be articulated and structured symbolically. The ideological and populist suggestions for solutions and harmony that are offered by Hollywood are only the one side; the other is the utopian or transcendent potential embodied in products of mass culture. Even the most shallow creations of mass culture still contain negative and critical elements that express antagonism toward the very social order whose commodified products they are. Otherwise they could not fulfill their ideological-manipulative function. They owe their attraction to the bribe they offer consumers in the currency of dreams. They legitimate the existing order, but in order to do so, they must express, at least in a rudimentary way, fears and resistance against what is, as well as the hope of surpassing it.

Since the 1960s, a critical theory of popular culture has established itself that rejects theories of manipulation, instead exploring how those making use of mass culture products alter their function in the process of using them. This research, bearing the general label of cultural studies, no longer starts from the assumption that a passive public submits to the culture of aestheticized commodities and identifies itself with what is offered. The model, rather, is a struggle for interpretive hegemony in the culture of daily life. It derives from Antonio Gramsci's understanding of hegemony as a complex mixture of compulsion and assent that a particular social group is able to enforce. In late-capitalist societies, the "power bloc" and "the people" stand opposed to each other. Jameson has summarized the new "conceptions of reading" of cultural texts, outlined by the cultural studies school, as "theories of resistance," theories about the "rewriting, appropriation of the commercial text by groups for whom it was not destined in that form." The extent to which cultural studies has changed perceptions has in recent years become especially vivid in German-speaking countries.

The project of a critical theory of society and culture is linked to the work of both Marx and Roland Barthes. For those studying the reception of mass media, mass communication is, in the Marxist sense, a relationship of production in which raw materials, namely, content, are imported, through encoding as information, into a commodity-based circle of exploitation. However, it is also the case that aesthetic use value undergoes complex subjective evaluations that cannot be reduced to their ideological-manipulative content. In *Myths of the Everyday*, Barthes formulates a structuralist semiotics of culture. He shows that cultural phenomena are organized like texts, that is, as sign-structures generating both denotations and connotations. In mass culture's media communication, the core meaning is overlaid with secondary components of meaning derived from connotations. The "mythologies" produced in this way are secondary sign-systems in which ideologies of everyday life are shaped; they cause social relations to appear as natural structures, and normally work with antithetical pairs of signs that exclude each other but appear together, like two sides of a coin. The conflicting meanings produce ambiguity. Even (or especially) with the most trivial objects, the semiotic multivalence of cultural texts can be decoded, and not only when it is generated by humor, irony, and metaphor.

Stuart Hall has argued that cultural texts can be decoded quite differently from the way they were encoded. Independent meanings can be achieved because different cultural users activate the text's levels of meaning in their own ways. The ability to recognize and decode multiple meanings is what defines aesthetic competence in the reading of mass culture. Stereotypical products can be received in individualizing ways contrary to their intentions. Obviously, increasing independence in reception, which makes old TV series such as *Dallas* or the 1960s German sci-fi production *Space Patrol* into cult objects today, is not necessarily an indicator of autonomy or freedom in the reception of commercial products. But such reception trajectories remain possible; the structural ambiguity of mass culture permits them. Indeed, that has long been acknowledged in specialized fields. Ambiguity no longer arises organically, but is manufactured. The fleeting interplay between explicit statements and latent meanings is planned. Again, Jameson's view is relevant: he insists on the fundamental difference between a critical theory of the culture industry and a theory of mass culture such as that advanced by cultural studies. He thinks it time to correct this discourse by means of a new "theory of manipulation" and a theory of "postmodern commodity universalism." While this is certainly important, in my view the productive aspects of mass culture, deriving from its ambivalent relationship to art, cannot be denied. Aesthetic experience is not defined only by specialists; today it is a means through which one understands oneself. A person's self-definition—as human, as man or woman, as member of a group or ethnicity, as a social and political being—is always also filtered through the articulation of needs and through the structuring of aesthetic competences. With their help, we can gain access to our own inner nature, as well as an understanding of what deprivation of such experiences means—that is, of how aesthetic competences can be blocked or suppressed. Popular cultural practice also includes a marking out of difference which, conversely, generates a sense of involvement in a particular discourse. As consumers of commodities and media, we are not passive victims of ideologies but are negotiating compromises between our own interests and what the consumer world is offering. The collaboration of media powers and their domination of public language make it ever harder for us to act autonomously. Yet methods of appropriation that counteract these difficulties—stubborn, self-defined forms of decoding—cannot be suppressed. As Adorno and Horkheimer stated in the 1947 edition of *Dialectic of Enlightenment*, the critical theory of mass culture is "to be continued."

Today both dimensions, critical theory and praxis, seem perhaps even more blocked than in Adorno's time. But to take that as a cause for resignation and bitterness would be to misunderstand Adorno. In his view, manipulation and compulsive conformity do indeed produce a "context of blindness," but not a determinism that would forever prevent that blindness from being destroyed. In *Minima Moralia*, the relevant epigram reads, "There is no true life within a false life." But that means there can be no true life for individuals, so long as the life of society as a whole is false. Only autonomous social praxis could counteract that trend. Adorno thought that a liberating praxis is today obstructed and blocked, and hence must be postponed, but not forever. In his pedagogical writings and conversations he argued for a "turn toward the subject" in order to prevent "the production of a true consciousness" as an educational goal from being forgotten, and in order to maintain the perspective of "the concept of an autonomous, mature human being capable of resisting the repetition of Auschwitz." In his sketches toward a negative moral philosophy, he wondered whether there could be, if not a "true" life, perhaps a "deputizing" life; whether it might be possible "to build, in the most intimate human relations, something like models for a true life." To do so would be to conduct one's affairs in the way "that one could imagine, on the basis of one's own experience, how the lives of liberated, peaceful and mutually supportive human beings should be structured." But Adorno had no illusions about this precarious, powerless concept of a life. As he writes in *Minima Moralia*, "There is no emancipation without that of society." However, lack of illusion does not mean lack of hope, not so long as philosophy and social theory make "the rescue of the hopeless" into their own cause.

Biographical Timeline

1903   Theodor Ludwig Wiesengrund-Adorno is born on September 11 in Frankfurt am Main. His father, Oscar Wiesengrund, is a wine merchant; his mother, Maria Wiesengrund (born Maria Calvelli-Adorno della Piana), is a singer.

1918   Beginning of friendship with Siegfried Kracauer.

1919   Attends the Hoch Music Conservatory in Frankfurt; studies composition with Bernhard Sekles and piano with Eduard Jung.

1921   Abitur at the Kaiser-Wilhelm Gymnasium in Frankfurt. Studies philosophy, sociology, psychology, and musicology at the University of Frankfurt. Begins work as a music critic. Becomes acquainted with Max Horkheimer.

1923   Meets Margarete Karplus and Walter Benjamin.

1924   Gains a doctorate in philosophy under supervision of Hans Cornelius. His dissertation is titled "The Transcendence of the Material and the Noematic in Husserl's Phenomenology."

1925	Studies composition with Alban Berg and piano with Eduard Steuermann in Vienna. Meets Arnold Schoenberg, Anton von Webern, Rudolf Kolisch, and Georg Lukács.
1927–28	Returns to Frankfurt. The study he has planned as a post-doctoral thesis (*Habilitationsschrift*), "The Concept of the Unconscious in Transcendental Spiritual Doctrine," is not submitted.
1928–31	Active as editor with the Viennese periodical *Dawn [Anbruch]: Austrian Music Journal*.
1931	Qualifies as lecturer (*Habilitation*) at the University of Frankfurt with his dissertation, supervised by Paul Tillich and titled "Kierkegaard's Construction of the Aesthetic." Inaugural lecture as instructor (*Privatdozent*) in philosophy.
1933	Publication of *Kierkegaard: Construction of the Aesthetic*. The Nazis withdraw his authorization to teach at the university and remove him from office.
1934	Exile in England. Residence as advanced student and instructor at Merton College, Oxford. Meets Karl Mannheim.
1937	Marriage to Dr. Margarete Karplus.
1938	Emigration to the United States. Joins the Institute for Social Research in New York. Directs the "Music Study" section of the Princeton Radio Research Project. Changes name to Theodor W. Adorno.
1941	Moves to Los Angeles. Intensive collaboration with Max Horkheimer on *Dialectic of Enlightenment*. Work on the philosophy of new music and *Minima Moralia*.
1943	Collaboration with Thomas Mann and Hanns Eisler.
1944	Contributes *Studies in Prejudice* to the Berkeley Project on the Nature and Extent of Anti-Semitism.
1947	Publication, with Max Horkheimer, of *Dialectic of Enlightenment*.

1949   Return to Frankfurt. Appointment as supernumerary professor of philosophy at the University of Frankfurt. Publication of *Philosophy of Modern Music*.

1950   Publication, with Else Frenkel-Brunswick et al., of *The Authoritarian Personality*. Re-establishment of the Institute for Social Research in Frankfurt; Adorno is the institute's acting director.

1951   Publication of *Minima Moralia: Reflections from Damaged Life*.

1952   Residence in the United States as scholarly head of the Hacker Foundation in Beverly Hills. Publication of *In Search of Wagner*.

1953   Return to Frankfurt. Appointment as extraordinary professor of social philosophy at the University of Frankfurt.

1954   Awarded the Arnold Schoenberg Medal.

1955   Publication of *Prisms*.

1956   Publication of *Against Epistemology* and *Dissonances*. Appointment as full professor of sociology and philosophy at the University of Frankfurt.

1958   Appointed, with Max Horkheimer, as director of the Institute for Social Research. Publication of *Notes to Literature*, vol. 1.

1959   Publication of *Sound Figures*, vol 1.

1960   Publication of *Mahler: A Musical Physiognomy*.

1961   Publication of *Notes to Literature*, vol 2.

1962   Publication of *Introduction to the Sociology of Music*, as well as *Soziologica II*. Gives lectures with Max Horkheimer.

1963   Elected president of the German Sociological Society. Awarded the Goethe Plaque by the city of Frankfurt. Publication of *Hegel: Three Studies*; *Interventions: Nine Critical Models*; *The Faithful Répétiteur: Teachings on Musical Practice*; and *Quasi una fantasia: Writings on Music*, vol. 2.

1964   Publication of *Musical Moments: Reprinted Essays, 1928–1962* and *The Jargon of Authenticity: On the German Ideology*.

1965   Publication of *Notes to Literature*, vol. 3.

1966   Publication of *Negative Dialectics*.

1967   Publication of *Without a Model: Aesthetic Impoverishment* [*Ohne Leitbild: Parva Aesthetica*].

1968   Publication of *Alban Berg: Master of the Smallest Link* and *Impromptus: Reprinted Musical Essays*, vol. 2.

1969   Publication, with Hanns Eisler, of *Composing for the Films*. Publication of *Keywords: Critical Models* and a new edition of *Dialectic of Enlightenment*. Publication, with coauthors, of *The Argument over Positivism in German Sociology*.

Adorno dies from a heart attack on August 6 in Visp, in the Swiss canton of Vallis.

Notes

1. The Project of Renewing Childhood
by Transforming One's Life

1. Both here and in other comments Thomas Mann played down the significance and breadth of Adorno's contribution to this great novel. A few years ago Rolf Tiedemann showed that Mann incorporated into the novel, word for word, texts that Adorno made available to him in Los Angeles. Possibly Mann later destroyed Adorno's original writings, since they are not to be found among his papers. However, it proved possible, in the Adorno archive in Frankfurt, to reconstruct Adorno's contributions word by word. The archive contains copies of those texts from his papers; evidently, Mann knew nothing of their existence. Adorno was hurt by the way Mann minimized his coauthorship of *Doktor Faustus*; however, he never demanded a formal correction from Mann and his family. Later, the correspondence between Mann and Adorno was published; from it one can reconstruct how Mann was inspired by Adorno's essay on Beethoven's late style and by his *Philosophy of Modern Music*—and how he might have been stimulated to quote from him without acknowledgment. Further, one can see how the theory of humanism's regression into mythology, developed in Horkheimer's and Adorno's *Dialectic of Enlightenment*, was transformed,

through the agency of Mann the "magician," into the motif of the composer Leverkühn who, at the height of musical modernity, "cancels" Beethoven's Ninth Symphony. The "'cancellation' of the Ninth means, if translated to Mann's own work, the cancellation of the four-part novel *Joseph and His Brothers*" (Marius Meller).

The later tensions between the two men do not reduce the value of Mann's biographical remarks about Adorno. These remarks refer also to Adorno's written texts; selections from them were subsequently included by Suhrkamp in a dossier accompanying the German publication of Adorno's *Collected Works*.

3. Reason's Self-Criticism

1. The inherently contradictory character of capitalist rationalism was first conceptualized by Georg Lukács in *History and Class Consciousness*, a work that was seminal for critical theory, with its critical philosophical interpretation of Marx. In the section of the book titled "Reification and the Consciousness of the Proletariat," Lukács writes,

> This apparently total rationalization of the world, reaching into the individual's deepest physical and psychic being, is ultimately limited by the formal character of its own rationality. That is, the rationalism of life's isolated elements and the resultant—formal—structures of coherence fit directly, when observed superficially, into a unified system of general "laws"; however, the disregard of the material basis supposedly governed by these laws, on which their "lawfulness" depends, becomes evident in the actual incoherence of the system of laws, in the randomness of the partial systems' relation to each other, and in the—relatively—substantial independence from each other possessed by these partial systems.

2. Furio Cerutti introduced the concept of "critical Marxism" to replace the "conventional expressions 'Hegelian Marxism' and 'Western Marxism,'" in order to "signal that what is involved in the works of these authors [Lukács and Korsch] is no mere restoration of Marxism's philosophical, i.e., Hegelian dimension; rather, the recourse to Hegel is linked directly with the rediscovery of the revolutionary, praxis-oriented, and critical content of Marxist theory."

3. In the first edition of *Dialectic of Enlightenment*, published in 1944, the authors use a terminology, oriented toward Marxist theory, that was partially replaced, in later editions, by "more neutral" concepts. The formulation cited here, "ratio of capital," is in the first edition an explana-

tory addition to the discussion of the "all-embracing ratio of an economic system that became irrational long ago." Willem van Reijen and Jan Bransen have investigated the textual changes that were made for the second edition, published in 1947. Their enlightening commentary, titled "Das Verschwinden der Klassengeschichte in der *Dialektik der Aufklärung*," appears as an appendix to the German edition of *Dialectic of Enlightenment* in Horkheimer's collected writings.

4. The authors point out that it is the shifting concept of necessity that causes the dialectical critique of enlightenment to oscillate between a finalist philosophy of history and a materialist theory of rupturing the continuum of history.

Do Horkheimer and Adorno think that necessity, when "clarified" into the stringency of formal logic, is merely another kind of mythical fate— or is something different from such a fate? The interpretation of their whole conception depends on this. Either they understand by "enlightenment" a law of movement that pervades history with the same irresistible necessity as Hegel's world spirit—except that its version of progress is not the direct "progress in the consciousness of freedom" that Hegel imagined, but one that complexity has turned into its opposite, with every step forward being simultaneously a step backward: a plunge deeper into the situation one longs to escape. Or they view this law of movement as a fate constructed by human beings, one that has grown, through its complexity, into a "natural" process that must be described and conceptualized if it is to be ruptured. There is no doubt that *Dialectic of Enlightenment*, in its overall impetus, aims at the latter outcome.

5. They are careful to avoid equating fundamentally different systems, a habit widespread during the Cold War and still common today.

4. Rescuing What is Beyond Hope

1. These considerations are to be understood in the context of an engagement, sometimes explicit, sometimes not, with Benjamin's thoughts on the theory of language, which were always important points of intellectual departure for Adorno.

5. The Totally Socialized Society

1. Elsewhere, however, in the *Aesthetic Theory*, he criticized this speech as imprecise:

What reading Shakespeare most clearly suggests is the dubiousness of the Marxian thesis that all history is the history of class struggle. . . . Objectively, class struggle presupposes a high level of social integration and differentiation; subjectively, a consciousness of class such as was developed, in rudimentary form, only in bourgeois society . . . social antagonisms are ancient; but before then they became class only occasionally, where a market economy akin to that of bourgeois society had been formed. Thus the interpretation of all history as class struggles has a slightly anachronistic quality, particularly since the model Marx used for construction and extrapolation was that of liberal enterprise capitalism.

2. Critical theory's Hegel-oriented philosophy of the individual is developed as a paradigm in Horkheimer's *Critique of Instrumental Reason*, in the chapter "Rise and Fall of the Individual."

3. An example: Adorno argues that Freud, even as he, while "in conflict with bourgeois ideology, materialistically tracked conscious behavior down to its unconscious source in psychic drives, at the same time concurred with the bourgeois contempt for these drives—a product of the very rationalizations he is deconstructing." Adorno bases this reproach on Freud's acknowledgment that he would rank social goals more highly than fundamentally selfish sexual goals. To conclude from that that psychoanalysis systemically despises drives is not convincing.

4. Alexander Mitscherlich has caricatured this objection as follows: "Political assembly on the large scale, arena filled to the last place, a carpet of people and faces in rising rows, the speaker is in full flood. He proclaims: 'Mass culture is to blame for everything.' Tidal wave of applause."

5. "The thesis of the disappearing individual," argues Detlev Claussen, "is in danger of interpreting a social tendency as a closed historical outcome. The priority of objective factors threatens to metamorphose into determinism, if the historical moment and constellation of social forces are not precisely defined."

6. Today we know better than the critical social theorists of that time how little the form of capitalism in the two decades after the Second World War could be called "late." At the same time, the distancing effect of this terminology must not make us forget that Adorno was no theorist of collapse in the "classical" sense. He did regard as valid the Marxian law of the tendential fall of profit rates, which could be halted only temporarily. But he refrained from any prognosis and from a more precise definition of the terms "tendential" and "temporary." Conversations with Fredric Jameson have led me to realize why Adorno's concept of "late capitalism" is so much

less problematic in the English-speaking world than in the German. It is connected to the double meaning of the English word "late": "late news" is not only broadcast late in the evening, but it is also the most recent news; and "late capitalism" can mean, in social-theoretical terms, "the most recent form of capitalism."

7. It is unclear why Anke Thyen at this point turns her vivid characterization of the goal of Adorno's concept of the nonidentical into a criticism of Adorno, with the cutting comment that Kant "already knew" it. It is no secret that Adorno's concept of the nonidentical, which is critical of Hegel, was generated by a highly idiosyncratic reading of Kant that never denied Adorno's experiences with neo-Kantianism; it is certainly not a secret that Adorno wanted to hide out of vanity. Perhaps Thyen has confused critical theory with academic philosophy: critical theory aims to articulate anew what it regards as the (partially discarded) truth content of tradition, whereas what matters most to academic philosophy are "original contributions" and "innovative readings"—useful for acquiring professorships and impressing colleagues at meetings.

6. The Goal of the Emancipated Society

1. Lukács claims that "the commodification of labor that is separated from the human being's total personality can only grow into a revolutionary class consciousness within the proletariat." He justifies this claim by arguing that employees who enter the bourgeoisie are also inwardly, spiritually integrated into the structure of class society, while proletarians become outwardly totally commodified, yet can resist the process subjectively. "The purely abstract negativity in the worker's existence is thus not only the most typical objective form of reification, the structural model for capitalist socialization, but also—for that very reason—the point where this structure can be raised to a conscious level, hence opened to practical rupture."

2. It is no accident that Adorno uses a literary text to develop his interpretation of the dialectics of progress, a text in which, as in the twelfth canto of the *Odyssey*, the metaphor of rowing is decisive. According to Horkheimer and Adorno in *Dialectic of Enlightenment*, in Homer the cunning of Odysseus, who can enjoy the pleasure of the Sirens' song because he has his men tie him to the mast—while their own ears are stuffed with wax—signifies "the fusion of myth, domination and labor." Even if only in an illusory, contemplative way, Odysseus can participate in the pleasure of

yielding to the dissociation from self promised by the Sirens' song, while simultaneously avoiding the danger of actually losing the self—as if he were the first bourgeois employing others to work for him. In Nietzsche's spirit, the authors contend that "humanity had to do dreadful things to itself until the self, the identity-based, purpose-driven, masculine individual character was created—and something of this is still repeated in every childhood. The effort to hold the self together inhibits the individual at every stage, and the temptation to abandon it was always inseparable from the blind resolve to maintain it."

7. The Powerless Utopia of Beauty

1. For Baumgarten, aesthetics becomes "a program for perfecting the human being's lower-level capacities for cognition, namely the senses. It is thereby opposed to logic as the discipline of rational cognition and does not, as is the case later with Kant, merely assume an auxiliary role in objective cognition. Aesthetics perceives other things and in a different way."

2. In contrast to the category of "content," for Adorno "material" means everything that "artists deploy: from words, colors, and sounds through linkages of all kinds to the complicated procedures for defining a whole work. In this sense forms can also become material; material is everything they confront about which they must make decisions."

3. "The expert . . . is definable through a fully competent hearing ability. He is the completely aware listener, who misses nothing of the development while fully registering, at every moment, what he is hearing. . . . Even as he spontaneously follows the movement of complex music, he is hearing the structural process, the fusion of past, present, and future moments, in such a way that a coherent meaning is crystallized from them. He even hears distinctly the differentiations within what is simultaneous, that is, complex harmonies and multiple voices. A completely adequate aesthetic response is definable as structural listening."

4. For Proust, Arnold Hauser writes,
time is no longer the principle of dissolution and destruction, no longer the element in which ideas and ideals lose value, and life and spirit lose substance; rather, it is the form in which we become conscious of and possess our spiritual being, our living self distinct from dead matter and mechanical processes. We are what we are not just in time but by means of time. We are not only the sum of our life's individual moments but the product of the qualities which these moments acquire through every new moment. We do not become poorer through time that is past and

"lost"; it is what fills our life with content. Proust's novel is the justification of Bergson's philosophy; only in Proust does Bergson's conception of time attain full validity. Existence gains life, motion, color, ideal transparency, and spiritual content only from the perspective of a present that is the product of our past. There is no other happiness than that of memory, of awakening, enlivening, and absorbing past and lost time.

5. Manuel Knoll summarized it thus: "For Adorno, philosophical truth is realized by the objectifying of the mimetically expressive moment of insight through language, or by making it binding through compelling articulation. Analogously, art gains its truth by objectifying its mimetically expressive moment through rational, constructive or formal coherence." For Wellmer, this construction has an aporetic basis in Adorno, since in his view the rational and sensuous experiences of aesthetic structures are not simply complementary with each other. The dynamic whereby rational and sensuous experiences repress each other leads Adorno to argue that artistic truth has a character that is at once obvious and elusive; in Wellmer's words:

> nondiscursive and discursive cognition both lay claim to the entirety of cognition, but precisely this split in the cognitive process means that each process can grasp only complementary refractions of truth. Combining these complementary refractions into a single, unabbreviated truth would be possible only if the split itself were overcome, if reality were reconciled. In the work of art, truth achieves a sensuous presence; that is what constitutes its priority over discursive cognition. But precisely *because* truth appears sensuously in art, it is once again masked from aesthetic experience; because the work of art cannot utter the truth that it manifests, aesthetic experience does not know what it is experiencing. The truth that reveals itself in the flash of aesthetic experience is simultaneously inaccessible as a concrete or actual truth. To clarify this linkage between the immediacy and the inaccessibility of the truth that appears aesthetically, Adorno compared works of art with puzzles and trick images.

6. In a 1932 address Lukács delivered on the Workers' Radio, titled "The Bourgeois Image of Goethe," he argues that the bourgeoisie is silent about the fact "that the 'Olympian' Goethe of the late period was also someone *resigned*":

> endeavoring to keep his private life to himself and, within this private world, to maintain and further develop the ideals of the progressive bourgeoisie. The weakness of the middle class at that time broke in two the development of the greatest German poet. . . . The revolutionary proletariat seeks to *learn dialectically* from the legacy of the progressive

moment in earlier years. It rejects categorically the position of Mehring, as if a Goethe falsified by the bourgeoisie could expect a restoration, a resurrection in socialist society. A restoration of Goethe means a restoration of the *contradictions of his class position*, the contradictory positions and solutions to which he had access on that basis. With this core premise, but *only* with this premise, Goethe is a very important element of that heritage to which the proletariat must gain access, must *assimilate for itself, in order to build a socialist culture.*

8. The Failure of Culture

1. Sven Kramer has pointed to the problematic element entailed by Adorno's constant references to "barbarism." The concept of barbarism bears the indelible trace of the ethnic as well as social repression in Adorno's historical roots. Adorno always used the concept in its everyday verbal sense, to designate the other of culture that is not only its other. One can draw attention to this need for terminological differentiation and avoid this traditional concept in one's own discussion of the issue. Adorno's treatment of the problem in his essay on Iphigenia shows unmistakably that he was far from sharing the arrogance of the educated bourgeoisie in relation to those who, either in fact or in the perspective of others, are untouched by culture.

2. Heinz Paetzold has shown that Adorno's dialectical critique of culture can be interpreted as an implicit engagement with the philosophies of culture of Ernst Cassirer and Georg Simmel.

3. As Detlev Claussen has written,
Critique of the culture industry, for Horkheimer, Adorno, Löwenthal, and Marcuse, meant a critical analysis of culture's commodity character, not a condemnation of commerce. With the term "culture industry" the authors designate the whole intricate web of cultural-industrial production and distribution and do not propose a culturally conservative legitimation of art as against mass culture. It is only the commodity character of culture that makes possible the appearance of autonomy in modern art; when it appeared in traditional art, the artists, as servant of feudal lords, saw it as a utopia. Bourgeois art is not celebrated by critical social theory as an autonomous sphere, but criticized as affirmative culture—which, however, now belongs to a past era.

4. As with Lyotard, whose postmodern aesthetic is really a late modern avant-garde aesthetic, so too for Adorno there are really only two options: avant-garde or kitsch.

Bibliography

Selected Works by Adorno in English

Adorno Reader, The. Edited by Brian O'Connor. Oxford: Blackwell, 2000.

Aesthetic Theory. Translated by Robert Hullot-Kentor and edited by Gretel Adorno and Rolf Tiedemann. Minneapolis: University of Minnesota Press, 1997.

Against Epistemology: A Metacritique; Studies in Husserl and the Phenomenological Antinomies. Translated by Willis Domingo. Cambridge, Mass.: MIT Press, 1983.

Alban Berg: Master of the Smallest Link. Translated by Juliane Brand and Christopher Hailey. New York: Cambridge University Press, 1991.

Aspects of Sociology, by the Frankfurt Institute for Social Research. Translated by John Viertel. Boston: Beacon Press, 1972.

Authoritarian Personality, The, by T. W. Adorno, Else Frenkel-Brunswik, Daniel J. Levinson, and R. Nevitt Sanford, in collaboration with Betty Aron, Maria Hertz Levinson, and William Morrow, in *Studies in Prejudice,* edited by Max Horkheimer and Samuel H. Flowerman. Vol. 1. New York: Harper and Brothers, 1950.

Beethoven: The Philosophy of Music; Fragments and Texts. Translated by Edmund Jephcott and edited by Rolf Tiedemann. Cambridge: Polity Press, 1998.

Can One Live After Auschwitz: A Philosophical Reader, by Theodor W. Adorno et al. Stanford, Calif.: Stanford University Press, 2003.

Composing for the Films, by Theodor W. Adorno with Hanns Eisler. New York: Oxford University Press, 1947.

Critical Models: Interventions and Catchwords. Translated by Henry W. Pickford. New York: Columbia University Press, 1998.

Culture Industry: Selected Essays on Mass Culture, The. Edited by J. M. Bernstein. London: Routledge, 1991.

Dialectic of Enlightenment: Philosophical Fragments, by Max Horkheimer and Theodor W. Adorno. Translated by Edmund Jephcott and edited by Gunzelin Schmid Noerr. Stanford, Calif.: Stanford University Press, 2002.

Essays on Music. Translated by Susan H. Gillespie and edited, with introduction, commentary, and notes, by Richard Leppert. Berkeley: University of California Press, 2002.

Hegel: Three Studies. Translated by Shierry Weber Nicholsen. Cambridge, Mass.: MIT Press, 1993.

In Search of Wagner. Translated by Rodney Livingstone. London: Verso, 1984.

Introduction to Sociology. Edited by Christoph Gödde and translated by Edmund Jephcott. Stanford, Calif.: Stanford University Press, 2000.

Introduction to the Sociology of Music. Translated by E. B. Ashton. New York: Continuum, 1988.

Jargon of Authenticity, The. Translated by Knut Tarnowski and Frederic Will. Evanston, Ill.: Northwestern University Press, 1973.

Kant's "Critique of Pure Reason." Translated by Rodney Livingstone and edited by Rolf Tiedemann. Stanford, Calif.: Stanford University Press, 2001.

Kierkegaard: Construction of the Aesthetic. Translated by Robert Hullot-Kentor. Minneapolis: University of Minnesota Press, 1989.

Mahler: A Musical Physiognomy. Translated by Edmund Jephcott. Chicago: University of Chicago Press, 1992.

Metaphysics: Concepts and Problems. Translated by Edmund Jephcott and edited by Rolf Tiedemann. Stanford, Calif.: Stanford University Press, 2000.

Minima Moralia: Reflections from Damaged Life. Translated by E. F. N. Jephcott. London: New Left Books, 1974.

Negative Dialectics. Translated by E. B. Ashton. New York: Continuum, 1983.

Notes to Literature. 2 vols. Translated by Shierry Weber Nicholsen and edited by Rolf Tiedemann. New York: Columbia University Press, 1991–92.

Philosophy of Modern Music. Translated by Anne G. Mitchell and Wesley V. Blomster. New York: Continuum, 1985.

Positivist Dispute in German Sociology, The, by Theodor W. Adorno et al. Translated by Glyn Adey and David Frisby. London: Heinemann, 1976.

Prisms. Translated by Samuel Weber and Shierry Weber. Cambridge, Mass.: MIT Press, 1981.

Problems of Moral Philosophy. Translated by Rodney Livingstone and edited by Thomas Schröder. Stanford, Calif.: Stanford University Press, 2000.

Psychological Technique of Martin Luther Thomas' Radio Addresses, The. Stanford, Calif.: Stanford University Press, 2000.

Quasi una fantasia: Essays on Modern Music. Translated by Rodney Livingstone. New York: Verso, 1992.

Sound Figures. Translated by Rodney Livingstone. Stanford, Calif.: Stanford University Press, 1999.

Stars Down to Earth, and Other Essays on the Irrational in Culture, The. Edited by Stephen Crook. New York: Routledge, 1994.

English Editions of Core Cited Twentieth-Century Texts

Barthes, Roland. *Mythologies*. New York: Hill and Wang, 1972.

Benjamin, Walter. *Illuminations*. Edited and with an introduction by Hannah Arendt. New York: Harcourt Brace Jovanovich, 1968. Includes "The Work of Art in the Age of Mechanical Reproduction" and "Theses on the Philosophy of History."

———. *One-Way Street and Other Writings*. London and New York: Verso, 1985.

Bloch, Ernst. *The Principle of Hope*. Cambridge, Mass.: MIT Press, 1986.

———. *The Spirit of Utopia*. Stanford, Calif.: Stanford University Press, 2000.

Bürger, Peter. *Theory of the Avant-garde*. Minneapolis: University of Minnesota Press, 1984.

Cassirer, Ernst. *Philosophy of Symbolic Forms*. New Haven, Conn.: Yale University Press, 1955.

Foucault, Michel. *Discipline and Punish: The Birth of the Prison.* New York: Random House, 1977.

Habermas, Jürgen. *The Structural Transformation of the Public Sphere: An Inquiry into the Category of Bourgeois Society.* Cambridge, Mass.: MIT Press, 1989.

———. *Theory of Communicative Action.* Cambridge, UK: Polity Press, 1984–87.

Hauser, Arnold. *The Sociology of Art.* New York: Routledge, 1982.

Horkheimer, Max. *Critical Theory.* New York: Seabury Press, 1972.

Kracauer, Siegfried. *Theory of Film: The Redemption of Physical Reality.* New York: Oxford University Press, 1960.

Löwenthal, Leo. *Literature, Popular Culture and Society.* Englewood Cliffs, N.J.: Prentice Hall, 1961.

Lukács, Georg. *History and Class Consciousness: Studies in Marxist Dialectics.* Cambridge, Mass.: MIT Press, 1970.

Lyotard, Jean-François. *The Postmodern Condition: A Report on Knowledge.* Minneapolis: University of Minnesota Press, 1984.

Mann, Thomas. *Doctor Faustus: The Life of German Composer Adrian Leverkühn as told by a Friend.* Translated by H. T. Lowe-Porter. New York: Alfred A. Knopf, 1948.

———. *The Story of a Novel: The Genesis of* Doctor Faustus. Translated by Richard and Clara Winston. New York: Alfred A. Knopf, 1961.

Marcuse, Herbert. *Negations.* Boston: Beacon Press, 1968.

Valéry, Paul. *Paul Valéry: An Anthology.* Princeton, N.J.: Princeton University Press, 1977.

Wellmer, Albrecht. *The Persistence of Modernity.* Cambridge, Mass.: MIT Press, 1991.

Selected Secondary Works on Adorno

Always, Joan. *Critical Theory and Political Possibilities: Conceptions of Emanicipatory Politics in the Works of Horkheimer, Adorno, Marcuse, and Habermas.* Westport, Conn.: Greenwood Press, 1995.

Bauer, Karin. *Adorno's Nietzschean Narratives: Critiques of Ideology, Readings of Wagner.* Albany: State University of New York Press, 1999.

Benhabib, Seyla. *Critique, Norm, and Utopia: A Study of the Foundations of Critical Theory.* New York: Columbia University Press, 1986.

Berman, Russell A. *Modern Culture and Critical Theory: Art, Politics, and the Legacy of the Frankfurt School.* Madison: University of Wisconsin Press, 1989.

Bernstein, J. M. *Adorno: Disenchantment and Ethics*. Cambridge: Cambridge University Press, 2001.
Brunkhorst, Hauke. *Adorno and Critical Theory*. Cardiff: University of Wales Press, 1999.
Buck-Morss, Susan. *The Origin of Negative Dialectics: Theodor W. Adorno, Walter Benjamin and the Frankfurt Institute*. New York: Free Press, 1977.
Burke, Donald A. *Adorno and the Need in Thinking: New Critical Essays*. Toronto: University of Toronto Press, 2007.
Claussen, Detlev. *Theodor W. Adorno: One Last Genius*. Cambridge, Mass.: Belknap Press of Harvard University Press, 2008.
Connell, Matt F. *Theodor W. Adorno: A Critical Primer*. London: Pluto Press, 2003.
Cook, Deborah. *Adorno, Habermas, and the Search for a Rational Society*. New York: Routledge, 2004.
———. *The Culture Industry Revisited: Theodor W. Adorno on Mass Culture*. Lanham, Md.: Rowman and Littlefield, 1996.
Cunningham, David, and Nigel Mapp. *Adorno and Literature*. New York: Continuum, 2006.
Delanty, Gerard. *Theodor W. Adorno*. Thousand Oaks, Calif.: SAGE, 2006.
Foster, Roger. *Adorno: The Recovery of Experience*. Albany: State University of New York Press, 2007.
Gerhardt, Christina. *Adorno and Ethics*. Durham, N.C.: Duke University Press, 2006.
Hammer, Espen. *Adorno and the Political*. New York: Routledge, 2006.
Hearfield, Colin. *Adorno and the Modern Ethos of Freedom*. Aldershot, U.K.: Ashgate, 2004.
Heberle, Renée. *Feminist Interpretations of Theodor Adorno*. University Park: Pennsylvania State University Press, 2006.
Hoeckner, Berthold. *Apparitions: New Perspectives on Adorno and Twentieth-Century Music*. New York: Taylor and Francis, 2006.
Hohendahl, Peter U. *Prismatic Thought: Theodor W. Adorno*. Lincoln: University of Nebraska Press, 1995.
Honneth, Axel. *The Critique of Power: Reflective Stages in a Critical Social Theory*. Translated by Kenneth Baynes. Cambridge, Mass.: MIT Press, 1991.
Huhn, Tom, ed. *The Cambridge Companion to Adorno*. Cambridge: Cambridge University Press, 2004.
Huhn, Tom, and Lambert Zuidervaart, ed. *The Semblance of Subjectivity:*

Essays on Adorno's Aesthetic Theory. Cambridge, Mass.: MIT Press, 1997.

Hullot-Kentor, Robert. *Things Beyond Resemblance: Collected Essays on Theodor W. Adorno.* New York: Columbia University Press, 2008.

Jäger, Lorenz. *Adorno: A Political Biography.* New Haven, Conn.: Yale University Press, 2004.

Jameson, Fredric. *Late Marxism: Adorno, or The Persistence of the Dialectic.* London: Verso, 1990.

Jarvis, Simon. *Adorno: A Critical Introduction.* New York: Routledge, 1998.

———. *Theodor Adorno.* London: Routledge, 2004.

———. *Theodor W. Adorno: Critical Evaluations in Cultural Theory.* London: Routledge, 2007.

Jay, Martin. *Adorno.* Cambridge, Mass.: Harvard University Press, 1984.

———. *The Dialectical Imagination.* 2nd ed. Berkeley: University of California Press, 1996.

Jenemann, David. *Adorno in America.* Minneapolis: University of Minnesota Press, 2007.

Lee, Lisa Yun. *Dialectics of the Body: Corporeality in the Philosophy of T. W. Adorno.* New York: Routledge, 2005.

Menke, Christoph. *The Sovereignty of Art: Aesthetic Negativity in Adorno and Derrida.* Translated by Neil Solomon. Cambridge, Mass.: MIT Press, 1998.

Morgan, Alastair. *Adorno's Concept of Life.* New York: Continuum, 2007.

Müller-Doohm, Stefan. *Adorno: A Biography.* Cambridge, UK: Polity Press, 2005.

Nicholsen, Shierry Weber. *Exact Imagination, Late Work: On Adorno's Aesthetics.* Cambridge, Mass.: MIT Press, 1997.

O'Connor, Brian. *Adorno.* Brussels: Revue Internationale de Philosophie, 2004.

———. *Adorno's Negative Dialectic: Philosophy and the Possibility of Critical Rationality.* Cambridge, Mass.: MIT Press, 2005.

Paddison, Max. *Adorno, Modernism and Mass Culture: Essays on Critical Theory and Music.* London: Kahn and Averill, 2004.

———. *Adorno's Aesthetics of Music.* New York: Cambridge University Press, 1993.

Pensky, Max, ed. *The Actuality of Adorno: Critical Essays on Adorno and the Postmodern.* Albany: State University of New York Press, 1997.

Plass, Ulrich. *Language and History in Theodor W. Adorno's "Notes to Literature."* New York: Routledge, 2007.

Rasmussen, David M., ed. *The Handbook of Critical Theory*. Oxford: Blackwell, 1996.

Rose, Gillian. *The Melancholy Science: An Introduction to the Thought of Theodor W. Adorno*. London: Macmillan, 1982.

Schmidt, James. *Theodor Adorno*. Aldershot, U.K.: Ashgate, 2007.

Schultz, Karla L. *Mimesis on the Move: Theodor W. Adorno's Concept of Imitation*. New York: Peter Lang, 1990.

Sherrat, Yvonne. *Adorno's Positive Dialectic*. Cambridge: Cambridge University Press, 2002.

Spitzer, Michael. *Music as Philosophy: Adorno and Beethoven's Late Style*. Bloomington: Indiana University Press, 2006.

Thomson, A. J. P. *Adorno: A Guide for the Perplexed*. New York: Continuum, 2006.

Van Reijen, Willem, et al. *Adorno: An Introduction*. Translated by Dieter Engelbrecht. Philadelphia: Pennbridge Books, 1992.

Wilson, Ross. *Theodor Adorno*. New York: Routledge, 2007.

Witkin, Robert W. *Adorno on Music*. New York: Routledge, 1998.

——. *Adorno on Popular Culture*. New York: Routledge, 2002.

Zuidervaart, Lambert. *Adorno's Aesthetic Theory: The Redemption of Illusion*. Cambridge, Mass.: MIT Press, 1991.

——. *Social Philosophy after Adorno*. New York: Cambridge University Press, 2007.

Index

Adenauer, Konrad, 8
administered society, the, 58–59, 72, 127, 133
aleatory style, 107–8
Antonioni, Michelangelo, 149
Aristotle, 21, 39, 49, 71
atonality, 106, 108, 127
Auschwitz, xi, 66–67, 132, 138–39, 143–44, 154, 158

Barthes, Roland, 156
Baudelaire, Charles, 97, 100, 147
Baumgarten, Alexander, 49, 96, 168
Beckett, Samuel, 76, 127, 134, 148
Beethoven, Ludwig van, 105, 150, 163–64
Benjamin, Walter, viii, xi, 2, 4, 9, 19, 28–29, 32, 35–36, 68, 87–88, 114, 120–31, 145

Berg, Alban, 3
Bergson, Henri, 110, 169
Bloch, Ernst, viii, 4, 58, 68, 78, 89, 92, 100
Borchardt, Rudolf, 30
Brecht, Bertolt, 19, 61, 120–21, 147
Boulez, Pierre, 106
Burckhardt, Jakob, 136–37

Cage, John, 107–8, 133
Cassirer, Ernst, 13, 75, 170
Cerutti, Furio, 164
Chaplin, Charles, 149
Claussen, Detlev, viii, 8, 32, 138, 166, 170
Coltrane, John, 112
commodification, 100, 106, 116, 118, 125, 128, 139, 142–43, 147, 150, 154–57, 170

Cornelius, Hans, 2
cult value, 121, 123
culture industry, 6, 111–18, 128, 134, 145–46, 149–57, 170

Darmstadt, 107
Doktor Faustus (Mann), 1, 6, 103–5, 108, 110, 133, 163
Durkheim, Emile, 114
Dutschke, Rudi, 8

Endgame (Beckett), 76, 148
Engels, Friedrich, 5
Erhard, Ludwig, 8
exhibition value, 121, 123

Feldman, Morton, 133
Feuerbach, Ludwig, 22–23
Flaubert, Gustave, 91
Fontane, Theodor, 113
Ford, Henry, 117
Foucault, Michel, 67, 73
Frankfurt Institute for Social Research, 2, 3, 5, 8, 16, 26, 32, 33, 60, 62, 66, 112–15, 118
Freud, Sigmund, viii, 64–66, 166
Frisch, Max, 140
Fromm, Erich, 4, 112, 117
futurism, 120

Gehlen, Arnold, 103
Gelb, Adhemar, 3
Goebbels, Joseph, 17
Goethe, Johann Wolfgang von, 129, 169–70
Goodman, Benny, 112
Gramsci, Antonio, 156
Gutzkow, Karl, 113

Haag, Karl-Heinz, 43–44
Habermas, Jürgen, 15, 16, 55, 130, 135

Hacks, Peter, 130
Hall, Stuart, 157
Hampton, Lionel, 112
Hauser, Arnold, 168
Hegel, Georg Wilhelm Friedrich, viii, xi, 13, 17, 20–25, 36, 38, 41, 88, 92, 95–99, 105, 107, 109, 112, 166–67
Heidegger, Martin, viii, 42, 69
Heraclitus, 97
Holocaust. *See* Auschwitz
Horkheimer, Max, 2–4, 6–8, 16, 17, 25–33, 45, 46, 55, 60, 61, 66, 83, 114–16, 118, 133, 145–47, 158, 163, 170
Hume, David, 50
Husserl, Edmund, vii, 38, 42, 109

Investigation, The, (Peter Weiss), 147

Jameson, Fredric, viii, 154–57, 166
jazz, 111–12, 149

Kafka, Franz, 91, 127, 134
Kagel, Mauricio, 107
Kant, Immanuel, vii–viii, xi, 2, 14, 24, 42–45, 70, 72–75, 86, 89, 94, 98–101, 105, 126, 153, 167
Karplus, Margarete, 5, 10, 71
Kästner, Erich, 12
Kierkegaard, Søren, viii, 4, 72
Klee, Paul, 29
Knoll, Manuel, 169
König, René, 55
Korngold, Erich Wolfgang, 132
Korsch, Karl, 81
Kracauer, Siegfried, 2, 4, 26–28, 96, 114, 120–25, 149
Krahl, Hans-Jürgen, 9

Kramer, Sven, 131, 170
Kranichstein, 107
Kriegel, Volker, 112

Lanzmann, Claude, 147
Le Corbusier, 69
Lenk, Kurt, 81, 111, 145
Ligeti, György, 108
Locke, John, 15
Lohmann, Hans-Martin, 64
Love Parades, 153
Löwenthal, Leo, 4, 31, 113–14, 170
Lukács, Georg, viii, 4, 81, 82, 124, 129–30, 164–67, 169
Lyotard, Jean-François, 95, 153–54, 170

Maase, Kaspar, 128
Mann, Thomas, 1–6, 103–5, 108, 110, 133, 163
Marcuse, Herbert, 4, 9, 114–15, 170
Marx, Karl, viii, xi, 3, 5, 15–18, 22–25, 32, 34, 37, 41, 51–57, 66, 72, 79–81, 83, 141, 156, 166
Marx Brothers, The, 117, 149
Maupassant, Guy de, 87
Mehring, Walter, 170
messianic theology, 35, 135
Mitscherlich, Alexander, 166
modernism, 2, 3, 68–69
Montesquieu, Charles, 153
Mozart, Wolfgang Amadeus, 131–32
Münchhausen, 143

Nietzsche, Friedrich, viii, xi, 30, 31, 40, 41, 46, 72, 74–75, 141, 168

objectification, 81–82, 101
Ohnesorg, Benno, 8

Paetzold, Heinz, 146, 170
Panofsky, Erwin, 124–25
Parker, Charlie, 112
Parmenides, 97
Picasso, Pablo, 134
Plato, 95–97
Poe, Edgar Allan, 147
Popper, Karl, 55
Porter, Cole, 95
Princeton Radio Research Project, 118
Proust, Marcel, 76, 91, 98, 110, 168–69

Rorty, Richard, 74

Schindler, Oskar, 147
Schlöndorff, 149
Schmitt, Carl, 73
Schnädelbach, Herbert, 14, 137
Schnitzler, Arthur, 113
Schoenberg, Arnold, 2, 106, 108
Scott, Walter, 150
serialism, 106, 108, 127
Shoah (Lanzmann), 147
Simmel, Georg, 170
Sitte, Willi, 130
Sobol, Joshua, 147
Sombart, Werner, 82
Soldier's Tale, The, (Stravinsky), 94
Sonneman, Ulrich, 130
Spengler, Oswald, 30, 141
Spielberg, Steven, 147
Springer, Axel, 9
Stendhal, 97, 100
Steuermann, Eduard, 3, 104
Stirner, Max, 60
Stockhausen, Karlheinz, 106
Stravinsky, Igor, 94
surplus value, 53, 56

Thyen, Anke, 167
Tiedemann, Rolf, 35, 163
Tübke, Werner, 130
twelve-tone system, 103–8

use value, 51, 52, 117, 150
utopia, utopian thinking, 48, 51, 59, 68, 72, 80, 89, 90, 115, 117, 120, 127, 134, 139, 154–55, 170

Valéry, Paul, 120
van Gogh, Vincent, 91, 94

Wagner, Richard, 132
Warner Brothers, 152
Webb, Chick, 112
Weber, Max, 18, 82–83, 102–3, 123
Weiss, Peter, 147
Wellmer, Albrecht, 129, 133, 135, 169
Whiteman, Paul, 111
Wiggershaus, Rolf, 119
Wilson, Teddy, 112
Wittgenstein, Ludwig, 47, 56
Wohlfarth, Irving, 32

Gerhard Schweppenhäuser is a professor of Design, Communication, and Media Theory at Würzburg. He has written many books expanding on the sociocultural, analytical mission of the Frankfurt School, including two that focus fully on Adorno: *Ethik nach Auschwitz: Adornos negative Moralphilosophie* (1993); *Soziologie im Späetkapitalismus: Zur Gesellschaftstheorie Th.W. Adornos* (1995).

James L. Rolleston is professor emeritus of Germanic languages and literatures at Duke University. He has written books on Kafka, Rilke, and on modern German poetry. His previous book-length translation of *Walter Benjamin: An Intellectual Biography*, by Bernd Witte (Wayne State University Press, 1991) won the German Literary Prize of the American Translators Association in 1993. He also published a translation of Peter Weiss's last play, *The New Trial*, with Duke University Press (2001).

Library of Congress Cataloging-in-Publication Data

Schweppenhäuser, Gerhard.
[Theodor W. Adorno zur Einführung. English]
Theodor W. Adorno : an introduction / Gerhard Schweppenhäuser ;
translated by James Rolleston.
p. cm.
Includes bibliographical references and index.
ISBN 978-0-8223-4454-4 (cloth : alk. paper)
ISBN 978-0-8223-4471-1 (pbk. : alk. paper)
1. Adorno, Theodor W., 1903–1969. I. Title.
B3199.A34S3813 2009
193—dc22   2008055239

www.ingramcontent.com/pod-product-compliance
Lightning Source LLC
Chambersburg PA
CBHW050243170426
43202CB00015B/2901